I 8/25/16

DESIGN, BUILD,
EXPERIMENT

Forensic Science Experiments

IN YOUR OWN

Crime Lab

ROBERT GARDNER

Enslow Publishing
101 W. 23rd Street
Suite 240
New York, NY 10011
USA

enslow.com

Published in 2016 by Enslow Publishing, LLC
101 W. 23rd Street, Suite 240, New York, NY 10011

Cataloging-in-Publication Data

Gardner, Robert.
  Forensic science experiments in your own crime lab / by Robert Gardner.
    p. cm. — (Design, build, experiment)
  Includes bibliographical references and index.
  ISBN 978-0-7660-6955-8 (library binding)
  1. Forensic sciences—Experiments—Juvenile literature. 2. Science projects—Juvenile literature. I. Gardner, Robert, 1929–   . II. Title.
  HV8073.8 G36 2016
  363.25—d23

Printed in the United States of America

To Our Readers: We have done our best to make sure all Web site addresses in this book were active and appropriate when we went to press. However, the author and the publisher have no control over and assume no liability for the material available on those Web sites or on any Web sites they may link to. Any comments or suggestions can be sent by e-mail to customerservice@enslow.com.

Portions of this book originally appeared in the book *Forenisc Science Projects With a Crime Lab You Can Build.*

Illustration credits: Jonathan Moreno; pialhovik/iStock/Thinkstock (graph paper background throughout book)

Photo credits: Enslow Publishing, LLC, pp. 13, 14, 15, 16, 18, 24, 28, 36, 39, 41, 44, 48, 51, 60, 69, 90, 95, 97, 100, 110, 115, 121; Hit1912/Shutterstock.com, p. 104; Jubal Harshaw/Shutterstock.com, p. 74; Science photo/Shutterstock.com, p. 88.

Cover illustrations: Olga Sapegina/Hemera/Thinkstock (student); Torsak Thammachote/Shutterstock.com (fingerprint).

Contents

Introduction 5

The Scientific Method 8

Safety First 9

Chapter 1. Building a Crime Lab 11

   1.1 Build Your Fingerprint Lab Station. 13

   1.2 Build Your Glass Analysis Lab Station 14

   1.3 Build Your Document Analysis Lab Station . . . 15

   1.4 Build Your Forensic Chemistry Lab Station . . . 16

Chapter 2. Some Crime-Solving Skills 17

   2.1 Sight Observations 18

   2.2 Observations with Your Other Senses. 19

⭐ 2.3 Testing Eyewitnesses. 21

   2.4 Testing Earwitnesses 23

Chapter 3. Prints and Imprints 24

   3.1 Recording Fingerprints. 25

⭐ 3.2 Classifying Fingerprints. 27

   3.3 Identifying Fingerprints 30

⭐ 3.4 Lifting Fingerprints. 31

⭐ 3.5 Viewing Latent Fingerprints 35

   3.6 Recording Lip Prints 38

   3.7 Casting Footprints. 40

   3.8 Studying Voiceprints 43

Chapter 4. Solving Crimes Using the
                Physical Sciences 45

   4.1 What Are These White Solids? 47

   4.2 Glass as Evidence 53

EXPERIMENTS WITH A ⭐ SYMBOL FEATURE IDEAS FOR YOUR SCIENCE FAIR.

★ 4.3 Density and Glass Evidence.................55
 4.4 Refractivity and Glass Evidence 59
★ 4.5 Refractivity by Immersion
     and Glass as Evidence 62

Chapter 5 Solving Crimes Using the
         Biological Sciences..................... 65
 5.1 Teeth Impressions...........................66
 5.2 Studying Bones to Solve Crimes 68
 5.3 Microbe Clues in Drowning Cases...........73
★ 5.4 Decomposition Clues 76
★ 5.5 Temperature and Time of Death............80
 5.6 DNA Evidence 89
 5.7 Blood Evidence..............................92
 5.8 Spatter Science: Blood Drops and Splashes..96
 5.9 Studying Hair Evidence......................99
 5.10 Studying Fiber Evidence 102

Chapter 6. Crimes With Documents............... 104
 6.1 Is It Real or Counterfeit? 105
 6.2 Indented Writing Evidence...................107
★ 6.3 Handwriting Evidence.......................109
 6.4 Ink Evidence.................................113
 6.5 Piecing It Back Together 117
 6.6 Using Invisible Inks..........................118
 6.7 Can You Break the Codes?...................120

     Answers to Some Questions in this Book.....122
     Appendix: Science Supply Companies........124
     Further Reading and Web Sites 125
     Index 126

EXPERIMENTS WITH A ★ SYMBOL FEATURE IDEAS FOR YOUR SCIENCE FAIR

Introduction

The science and scientific techniques used to solve crimes are called forensic science. It is often used in courts to prove the guilt of a person accused of a crime. But it can also be used to prove a person's innocence. For example, a number of people put in prison have later been released. They were convicted before DNA testing was developed. Once DNA testing became available, it proved their innocence.

Edmond Locard (1877–1966), a French criminalist, is regarded by many as the father of forensic science. Locard proposed that every criminal leaves something at the scene of his crime and carries away something from that crime. The things left or taken often provide the evidence needed to convict the guilty person. According to Locard, "Every contact leaves a trace."

Using this book you can build your own crime lab. It will contain some of the items used by forensic scientists to help solve crimes. If you find that you enjoy this type of science, you may have discovered your future occupation. Many colleges offer courses in forensic science that can lead to a great career.

At times, you may need a partner. You should work with someone who enjoys experimenting and solving crimes as much as you do. In that way, you will both enjoy what you are doing. **This book will alert you to any danger involved in doing an experiment. In some cases, to avoid danger, you will be asked to work with an adult. Please do so.** Do not take any chances that could lead to an injury.

Like any good scientist, you should record your ideas, notes, data, and anything you can conclude from your investigations in a notebook. By so doing, you can keep track of the information you gather and the conclusions you reach. It will allow you to refer to things you have done and help you in doing other projects in the future.

SCIENCE FAIRS

Some of the investigations in this book contain ideas you might use at a science fair. Those projects are indicated with a ⚝ symbol. However, judges at science fairs do not reward projects that are simply copied from a book. For example, sample fingerprints of different people would not impress most judges; however, using those fingerprints to establish the percentage of people with certain fingerprint patterns or developing techniques to lift (remove) fingerprints from surfaces would be more likely to attract their attention.

Science fair judges tend to reward creative thought and imagination. It is difficult to be creative or imaginative unless you are really interested in your project; therefore, try to choose an investigation that appeals to you. Before you jump into a project, consider, too, your own talents and the cost of the materials you will need.

If you decide to use an experiment or idea found in this book for a science fair, you should find ways to modify or extend it. This should not be difficult because you will discover that new ideas come to mind as you carry out investigations. Ideas will come to you that could make excellent science fair projects, particularly because the ideas are your own and are interesting to you.

If you decide to enter a science fair and have never done so, you should read some of the books listed in the "Further Reading" section. These books deal specifically with science fairs and provide plenty of hints and useful information that will help you avoid pitfalls that sometimes plague first-time entrants. You will learn how to prepare appealing reports that include charts and graphs, how to set up and display your work, how to present your project, and how to talk to judges and visitors.

THE SCIENTIFIC METHOD

When you do a science project, especially one with your own original research, you will need to use what is commonly called the scientific method. In many textbooks you will find a section devoted to the subject. The scientific method consists of a series of steps.

1. Come up with a **QUESTION** or try to solve a **PROBLEM**. What are you curious about?

2. **RESEARCH** your topic. Find out what is already known. Has anyone already answered your question or solved your problem? What facts are published about your topic?

3. Form a **HYPOTHESIS**, which is an answer to your question or a solution to your problem.

4. Design an **EXPERIMENT** to test your hypothesis. Collect and record the data from your experiment.

5. Study your experimental **RESULTS** and form a **CONCLUSION**. Was your hypothesis true or false?

6. **REPORT** your findings.

Many scientists will tell you that each investigation is unique and requires different techniques, procedures, and ways of thinking. All good scientific projects try to answer a question, such as "Do identical twins have identical fingerprints?" Once you have a question, you will need to form a hypothesis. Perhaps you think that identical twins do have identical fingerprints. Your experiment should then test your hypothesis.

Scientific reports are very similar in format and include the problem, the hypothesis, the experimental procedure, the results, and a conclusion. You will follow a similar format when you prepare the report for your project.

SAFETY FIRST

Most of the projects included in this book are perfectly safe. However, the following safety rules are well worth reading before you start any project. Whenever doing chemistry experiments, it is a good idea to **wear safety glasses**. Most of the substances are not dangerous, but they might sting your eyes if they splatter.

1. Do any experiments or projects, whether from this book or of your own design, under the supervision of a science teacher or other knowledgeable adult.

2. Read all instructions carefully before proceeding with a project. If you have questions, check with your supervisor before going any further.

3. Maintain a serious attitude while conducting experiments. Fooling around is dangerous to you and to others.

4. Wear approved safety goggles when you are working with a flame or doing anything that might cause injury to your eyes.

5. Have a first-aid kit nearby while you are experimenting.

6. Do not put your fingers or any object other than properly designed electrical connectors into electrical outlets.

7. Never let water droplets come in contact with a hot light bulb.

8. Never experiment with household electricity.

9. Use only alcohol-based thermometers. The liquid in some thermometers is mercury. It is dangerous to breathe mercury vapor, and such thermometers have been banned in many states. When doing these experiments, use only nonmercury thermometers, such as those filled with alcohol. If you have a mercury thermometer in the house, **ask an adult** if it can be taken to a local mercury thermometer exchange location.

CHAPTER 1

Building a Crime Lab

A forensic scientist is responsible to examining and analyzing the evidence from a crime scene. They do much of this work in a laboratory. Their work requires chemicals, equipment, and a variety of materials. In this chapter, you will gather most of the things you need to build your crime lab. You will then be ready to carry out the forensic science experiments found in this book. After you complete some or all of these investigations, you may want to carry out more. If you do, you can always add things to your laboratory.

Crime labs have spaces where equipment, chemicals, and other materials are kept. Ask a parent or guardian if you can use shelves and boxes in your basement, garage, or bedroom to store your crime lab equipment. Also, ask if you can do some experiments in the kitchen. A kitchen is a good place to carry out tests and experiments. It provides access to a sink, water, counter space, a heat source (stove), a refrigerator, and a freezer. These are all items that would be found in most crime labs.

STARTING TO SET UP A CRIME LAB

Much of the materials and equipment you will need can be found in your home, borrowed from your school, purchased from local stores, or ordered from one of the science supply companies listed in the appendix.

You will need a variety of chemicals and materials as you examine evidence. In this chapter you can set up a number of laboratory stations that you will use later as you do the investigations that follow. A few additional materials that you may need for some of the experiments will be listed under *You Will Need* at the beginning of each investigation. You should always have a notebook and a pen or pencil at your side.

You can set up lab stations where you can examine and lift fingerprints, analyze documents or glass samples, and where you can find the chemicals commonly needed by forensic scientists. If you gather these materials now, you will be ready to work on the investigations and experiments in Chapters 2 through 6.

Build Your
Fingerprint Lab Station

You will investigate fingerprints and other prints in Chapter 3. Gather the following materials to set up a fingerprint lab station. Place the materials in a box labeled "Fingerprints and Other Prints."

YOU WILL NEED

- INK PAD
- PEN
- PENCIL WITH SOFT LEAD (GRAPHITE)
- MAGNIFYING GLASS (HAND LENS)
- SHEETS OF WHITE PAPER
- BLACK INK (FOR INK PAD)
- SOFT CLAY OR PLASTICINE
- COOKING OIL
- MICROSCOPE SLIDES
- WINDOW GLASS OR GLASS PLATE
- CAMERA (OPTIONAL)
- DOWNY FEATHER OR SOFT COTTON
- ALUMINUM FOIL
- BABY POWDER, TALCUM POWDER, GRAPHITE POWDER, OR CORNSTARCH
- DARK LIPSTICK
- PLASTER OF PARIS
- LARGE PAPER CUP
- CLEAR, WIDE PLASTIC TAPE
- NINHYDRIN POWDER (OPTIONAL)
- SUPER GLUE
- SMALL PLASTIC BOX THAT CAN BE SEALED (SOME TOOTHPICKS ARE SOLD IN SUCH CONTAINERS)

Build Your Glass Analysis Lab Station

In Chapter 4 you will investigate the ways that forensic science uses glass evidence. Collect the following materials to set up a glass analysis lab station. Place the materials in a box labeled "Glass Analysis."

You Will Need

- SMALL GLASS JARS
- METRIC BALANCE
- METRIC MEASURING CUP
- LARGE JAR
- KOSHER SALT
- COFFEE STIRRER
- DROPPER
- CLEAR GLASS OR PLASTIC JAR
- METAL SPOON
- WHITE PAPER
- COMB
- FLASHLIGHT
- GLASS PRISM
- TRANSPARENT PLASTIC TAPE
- LIGHT-COLORED COOKING OIL
- CLEAN GLASS OR BEAKER
- GLASS STIRRING ROD (OPTIONAL)

Build Your Document Analysis Lab Station

You will investigate documents associated with crimes in Chapter 6. Use the following materials to set up a document analysis lab station. Place the materials in a box labeled "Document Analysis."

YOU WILL NEED

- STRONG MAGNIFYING LENS OR MICROSCOPE
- ERASER
- DROPPER
- BLEACH
- BALLPOINT PEN
- PAD OF PAPER
- PENCIL WITH SOFT LEAD
- MARKING PENS OF DIFFERENT COLORS
- BLUE AND BLACK INK PENS
- SCISSORS
- PENCILS
- TINCTURE OF IODINE
- WHITE COFFEE FILTERS, FILTER PAPER, OR BLOTTER PAPER
- FOOD COLORINGS (OPTIONAL)
- ALUMINUM FOIL
- RUBBING ALCOHOL
- SHARP KNIFE
- TOOTHPICKS
- LEMON JUICE
- WHITE PAPER
- SAUCER
- OLD NEWSPAPER

Build Your Forensic Chemistry Lab Station

Use the following chemicals and related items to carry out the chemical experiments and tests you can do in this book. Be sure that the chemicals are properly labeled. Place them on a shelf or table labeled "Forensic Science Chemicals."

If you wish, all the chemicals found in the other lab stations can be stored at this station.

YOU WILL NEED

- CORNSTARCH
- WHITE FLOUR
- SUGAR
- BAKING SODA
- KOSHER SALT
- PLASTIC MEDICINE CUPS OR VIALS
- TINCTURE OF IODINE
- LIGHT-COLORED COOKING OIL
- ALCOHOL-BASED THERMOMETER WITH A RANGE OF -10°C–110°C OR 0°F–220°F
- GRAPH PAPER
- METRIC MEASURING CUP OR GRADUATED CYLINDER
- STYROFOAM CUPS
- TWEEZERS

CHAPTER 2

Some Crime-Solving Skills

How tall was the person at the crime scene? What color hair did she have? Was the car light blue or light green? When things happen quickly and during an accident or a crime, it may be difficult for most witnesses to accurately remember everything they see.

Like all professionals, criminalists (people who solve crimes) have to develop certain skills. They need trained and skilled observational skills. In this chapter you will test your observational skills using sight, smell, touch, and hearing. You will also carry out experiments to see whether evidence provided by eyewitnesses and earwitnesses can be trusted.

Sight
Observations

Successful forensic scientists and detectives have keen observational skills. They often find things at a crime scene that are unusual or that might serve as valuable evidence.

To test your own observational skills, look at the baseball players in Figure 1. How many errors can you detect in the drawing? In your science notebook, write down all the errors you can find. Then compare your list with the list on page 122.

FIGURE 1: The drawing shows a pitcher, batter, and catcher. How many "errors" do you see?

Observations with Your Other Senses

In the previous experiment, you observed with your eyes. But analyzing evidence often depends on senses other than sight, such as touch, hearing, and smell. A criminalist might also use taste, but **you should not taste substances unless you know they are safe.**

1. To test how well you and a fellow crime-solver use your senses, prepare a box that contains a number of objects. You might include an apple or an orange, a pencil, a bar of fragrant soap, a paper towel, a tennis or baseball, an eraser, a paper clip, a small toy, a plastic lid, a rubber band, a baby's rattle, or other items.

YOU WILL NEED

- BOX
- VARIETY OF OBJECTS SUCH AS FRUIT, A PENCIL, FRAGRANT SOAP, PAPER TOWEL, TENNIS OR BASEBALL, ERASER, PAPER CLIP, SMALL TOY, PLASTIC LID, RUBBER BAND, BABY'S RATTLE, OR OTHER ITEMS
- A FRIEND
- BLINDFOLD
- BENCH IN A PARK OR ON A CITY STREET
- NOTEBOOK
- PEN OR PENCIL
- TAPE RECORDER AND CASSETTE TAPES

2. Hand the box to another crime-solver who is blindfolded. Can he or she identify anything in the box by smell? How many of the items can he or she identify by touch? By sound?

3. Now have the crime-solver you tested prepare a box of items for you to identify. How many items could you identify by smell? By touch? By sound?

4. To further test your ability to observe by using sound, sit on a bench in a park or on a city street. Close your eyes and listen. How many different sounds do you hear? For how many can you identify the source? Can you tell the difference between a car horn and a truck horn? If you hear footsteps, are they a child's or an adult's? Are they made by someone wearing high heels? With leather soles or rubber soles? What other sounds can you identify?

5. Record a variety of sounds such as running water, a dog drinking water, rain falling on a roof, a creaking door, someone sawing a board, a carpenter driving nails, an automobile motor, and so on. How many sounds can your fellow criminalist identify?

6. Have someone make a similar recording. How many of the sounds can you identify?

Testing Eyewitnesses

After a crime has been committed, investigators interview people who may have witnessed the crime. If more than one witness observed a crime, all are interviewed to see if their observations agree. You can do something similar.

YOU WILL NEED

- COOPERATIVE TEACHER
- CLASSMATES
- FRIEND, SIBLING, OR PARENT
- MASK
- CLASSROOM
- WALLET
- PAPER AND PENCILS

1. Ask a teacher if he or she will let you stage a mock crime as an experiment to see how well eyewitnesses remember what they see at a crime scene. Have the teacher alert your classmates that this will happen at some point during the class so that they will not be afraid when it happens.

2. Have a masked friend, sibling, or parent come into the classroom, put a finger to the lips to signal silence, and then take your wallet, which you have conveniently placed on your desk. To make the "robber's" task easier, plan to be away from your desk when you know the "crime" is about to be committed.

3. After the "robber" leaves the room, ask each eyewitness to write answers to the following questions: How old was the robber? Approximately how tall was the robber? How much did the robber weigh? What was the color of the robber's hair? What was the robber's skin color? Was the robber African American, Hispanic, Caucasian, or Asian? What was the robber wearing? Did the robber have a gun? Did the robber have any scars or distinguishing features? What else did you notice?

4. Collect the answers to these questions and compare them. Did all the witnesses give similar answers? What can you conclude about eyewitness accounts?

Eyewitness accounts are often seen as solid evidence by jurors. Unfortunately, as you have probably learned from your experiment, eyewitness accounts are less reliable than people believe. They are based on the memory of an event that may have taken place some time ago. Furthermore, a lawyer's probing questions; newspaper, radio, and television reports; and personal bias can alter a witness's memory.

IDEA FOR YOUR SCIENCE FAIR

Ask the same people to answer the same questions a day later and a week later. How do their answers compare? How does time affect their eyewitness accounts?

Testing Earwitnesses

Witnesses also may be asked to identify a criminal as an "earwitness" instead of an eyewitness. For example, it may have been so dark that witnesses could not see, but they may have heard a criminal speak. Or a witness may have received a threatening phone call.

1. When friends call you on the telephone, do you always recognize their voices? Ask a friend to disguise his or her voice when calling you. Can your caller make you think someone else is calling? Can you do the same to your friend?

2. Now you need a room with a number of people in it, such as a family gathering or a classroom of students. Stand outside the room. One person in the room will say, "How are you?"

3. Go into the room and ask each person to say, "How are you?" Can you identify the person who spoke when you were out of the room? Is it easier to identify the voice if you know the people involved?

Do you think the testimony of earwitnesses should be considered as convincing evidence in court?

CHAPTER 3

Prints and Imprints

Criminals always carry their fingerprints to the scenes of their crimes. Often, they also leave them behind. Fingerprints are valuable clues in solving crimes because no two people, not even identical twins, have the same fingerprints. But, as you will see, fingerprints are not the only prints criminals leave at crime scenes.

Name:				
Right Hand				
Left Hand				

TABLE 1: Fingerprint Record

Recording Fingerprints

You can see your fingerprints, the tiny ridges in the skin covering your fingertips. Look at your fingertips in strong light. The fine pattern of ridges you see were with you at birth. They will remain unchanged, unless scarred, throughout your life. Your fingertips contain thousands of sweat pores that carry body oils to the ends of your fingers. When you touch something, the oils on the ridges leave their unique pattern on whatever you touch. That is why thieves often wear gloves.

YOU WILL NEED

- INK PAD
- PENCIL WITH SOFT LEAD (GRAPHITE)
- WHITE PAPER
- PEN
- PEOPLE WHO AGREE TO BE FINGERPRINTED
- TAPE

1. To record a set of fingerprints, you need an ink pad, a sheet of white paper, and a pen. The paper can be labeled as shown in Table 1. Ask a friend for permission to take his or her fingerprints. Hold the top half of the finger to be printed with both your hands. Roll the last (end) joint of the finger along an ink pad. Be sure the finger does not slip. If it does,

the print will be smudged. Using the same motion, roll the inked finger along a sheet of paper. All the prints should reveal the fingerprint patterns as clearly as possible. You may want to practice the procedure a few times until you can do it confidently.

If you do not have an ink pad, use graphite. Rub the fingertips with the side of a pencil that has very soft lead (graphite) such as a #2B. Then place the sticky side of a piece of wide, clear tape on the fingertip. When you remove the tape, the fingerprint will be on the tape. The on-tape print can then be stuck onto the proper place on the labeled paper.

2. Record the fingerprints of as many people as agree to be fingerprinted. Have one of your volunteers record your fingerprints.

Classifying Fingerprints

1. Using a magnifier, examine each of the fingerprint records you made in the previous experiment. Figure 2a shows the four basic patterns found in fingerprints: arches, loops, whorls, and combinations. In an arch pattern the ridge lines begin on one side of the finger, rise, and then decline as they move toward the other side of the finger. With a loop pattern, the ridge lines start and end on the same side of the finger. Whorls are circular patterns that do not begin or end on either side of the finger.

YOU WILL NEED

- FINGERPRINT RECORDS FROM PREVIOUS EXPERIMENT
- MAGNIFIER
- PEN OR PENCIL

2. Label each fingerprint as A (for arch), L (for loop), W (for whorl), and C (for a combination of basic patterns). Continue to examine the prints with a magnifier. Look for details within the print. Some of the details you may find are shown in Figure 2b. Record any details you find beside the appropriate print.

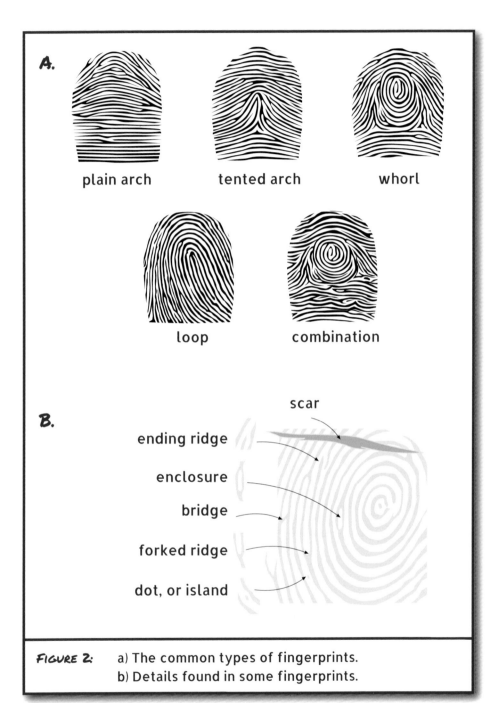

A.

plain arch   tented arch   whorl

loop   combination

B.

scar

ending ridge

enclosure

bridge

forked ridge

dot, or island

FIGURE 2:   a) The common types of fingerprints.
             b) Details found in some fingerprints.

A fingerprint found at a crime scene is often incomplete. Fingerprint experts require 12 to 15 points of similarity between two fingerprints to consider it a match. But for a forensic scientist to search fingerprint records looking for a match would be a time-consuming process. Fortunately, police have access to the Federal Bureau of Investigation's (FBI's) automated fingerprints identification system (AFIS). AFIS is a computerized database that contains 47 million fingerprint records. AFIS can search for a match to a fingerprint at a rate of 1,200 per second. If the computer identifies several possible matches, a fingerprint expert examines the prints carefully and decides whether the prints really match.

Ideas for your Science Fair

- What percentage of fingerprints are of the arch type? Loop type? Whorl type? Combination?
- Why are fingerprints always taken from the last joint of the fingers?

Identifying Fingerprints

Sometimes fingerprints are visible and easily photographed. The fingers that made them were dirty, greasy, bloody, or covered with some other matter such as paint. Other fingerprints are plastic; that is, they are seen as an impression in clay, in paint that was wet, in glue or chocolate that was soft, or in some other substance.

You Will Need

- PEOPLE FOR WHOM YOU HAVE FINGERPRINT RECORDS FROM EXPERIMENT 3.1
- PAPER
- INK, SOOT, OR DIRT
- SOFT CLAY

Ask some of the people for whom you have fingerprint records to choose one of them to leave visible fingerprints on a piece of paper. The volunteer can cover a finger with ink, soot, or dirt before leaving a distinct fingerprint. Have another person from the group leave a fingerprint in soft clay. Your task is to examine the prints and see if you can identify the "suspect."

Lifting Fingerprints

As you have seen, fingerprints are sometimes visible; however, more commonly, fingerprints are latent. That is, they are not easily seen. They require some treatment in order to be seen and analyzed.

You can make a latent fingerprint, make it visible, and remove (lift) it for examination. The pattern in a latent fingerprint is caused by the natural oils on human skin. When you touch something, the oils on the ridges of your fingertips leave a pattern on whatever you touch.

You Will Need

- A FRIEND
- FINGERPRINTS FROM EXPERIMENT 3.1
- MICROSCOPE SLIDE OR GLASS PLATE
- GRAPHITE POWDER, BABY POWDER, TALCUM POWDER, OR CORNSTARCH
- DOWNY FEATHER OR SOFT COTTON
- CAMERA (OPTIONAL)
- CLEAR PLASTIC TAPE, WIDE
- NINHYDRIN POWDER (OPTIONAL)
- PAPER

1. Have a friend, whose fingerprints you have on file, rub his thumb on his forehead, then press the thumb on a microscope

slide or glass plate. You may be able to see the fingerprint if you observe it at just the right angle.

2. To lift the fingerprint, you must first dust it. Dusting a fingerprint is a very delicate process. To begin, sprinkle a small amount of graphite powder, baby powder, talcum powder, or cornstarch on the surface near the print. Then use a soft, downy feather or a few wisps of soft cotton to spread the powder over the print. The brushing must be done with a very soft material. A watercolor paint brush is too coarse.

3. If you succeed in making the print visible, you might like to take a photograph if you have a camera that can get a close-up view. Then lift the print. Carefully place the sticky side of a wide piece of clear plastic tape over the print. Do not touch the sticky part of the tape that will go over the fingerprint. When you peel the tape away, the fingerprint will come with it. The fingerprint can then be taped to a piece of paper.

4. Compare the lifted fingerprint with the one you recorded earlier. Can you see that the two fingerprints match?

5. Practice lifting fingerprints until you master the technique. Then try dusting and lifting fingerprints from different hard surfaces. Can you identify the people who made them?

6. The police often use ninhydrin powder to reveal fingerprints

left on paper. If your school's science department has ninhydrin powder, you might ask to use some. Be patient. It takes a day or two for prints dusted with ninhydrin to become visible. Can you identify the source of the fingerprints?

Recently, police have been using diazafluoren (DFO) rather than ninhydrin to make latent prints visible. They also use silver nitrate ($AgNO_3$) solutions, which react with the salt (NaCl) in the sweat left by fingers to form silver chloride (AgCl). The print must then be exposed to ultraviolet light to form silver, leaving a black or reddish brown print.

Forensic scientists sometimes use iodine fumes to make fingerprints visible. The violet **vapors of iodine are poisonous, so you should not use this technique**, which must be done in a fume hood. By placing a paper suspected of having fingerprints in the iodine's violet vapor, forensic scientists can see crystals of iodine form along the pattern of ridge lines in the fingerprints.

Although you will not be using iodine, you can investigate a similar method using cyanoacrylate (Super Glue) in the next experiment. It is very useful in making visible latent prints on aluminum foil and plastics.

IDEAS FOR YOUR SCIENCE FAIR

- Make latent fingerprints on different surfaces. You might try glass, formica, metal, wood, paper, linoleum, cloth, and so on. On which surfaces are fingerprints clearest? On which surfaces are they faintest?

- How can fingerprints be lifted from a window?

- Do any animals have "fingerprints?"

Viewing Latent Fingerprints

1. Find a small plastic box that can be sealed. Then ask an adult to help you with this experiment. Rub the tip of your index finger along your forehead. Use that finger to make a fingerprint on a small piece of aluminum foil.

2. Being careful not to touch the fingerprint, tape the foil to the top inside surface of the box's lid as shown in Figure 3a. The side of the foil with the fingerprint should be exposed.

3. Fold another small piece of aluminum foil to make a little pan. Put it on the bottom of the box.

4. **Ask an adult** to squeeze some Super Glue into the little pan. **Do not get Super Glue on your fingers.** It bonds everything it touches!

5. Seal the box (Figure 3b) with clear tape. The cyanoacrylate vapor will slowly condense on the oils along the ridges of the

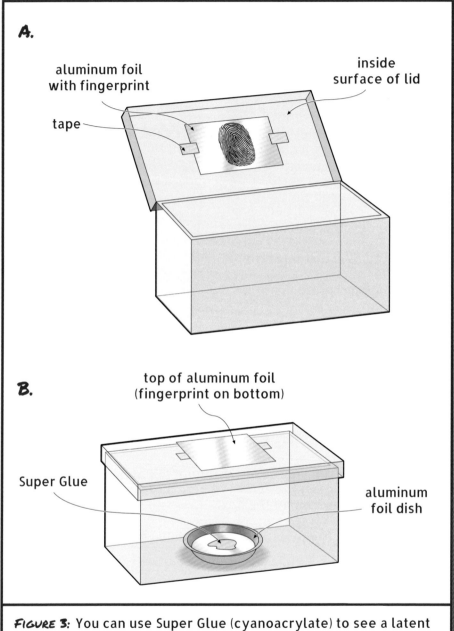

A.

aluminum foil with fingerprint

inside surface of lid

tape

B.

top of aluminum foil (fingerprint on bottom)

Super Glue

aluminum foil dish

FIGURE 3: You can use Super Glue (cyanoacrylate) to see a latent fingerprint.

fingerprint. Allow four to five hours for the grayish-white print to develop.

IDEAS FOR YOUR SCIENCE FAIR

- Collect fingerprints and toeprints from a friend or a family member. Do toeprints and fingerprints match? Are the same arch, loop, and whorl patterns found in toeprints?
- Fingerprints are the pattern of ridges on your fingertips. Do these ridges serve any useful purpose?

Recording Lip Prints

Lip prints are often seen on glasses from which people wearing lipstick have drunk.

YOU WILL NEED

- DARK LIPSTICK
- WHITE PAPER
- PEOPLE FROM WHOM YOU CAN COLLECT LIP PRINTS
- CLEAR TAPE
- DRINKING GLASSES
- FACIAL TISSUE

1. To make a lip print, rub a dark lipstick onto your lips. Rub your lips together to spread the color evenly.

2. Fold a sheet of white paper. Put the folded paper between your lips. Press your lips firmly against the paper. Do not smudge the print by sliding your lips along the paper.

Figure 4 shows the common patterns seen in lip prints; however, many people have mixed lip patterns. What pattern or patterns do you see in your own lip prints?

3. Collect and record the lip prints of as many people as possible. Are lip prints as unique as fingerprints? Can you use clear tape to lift lip prints from a glass?

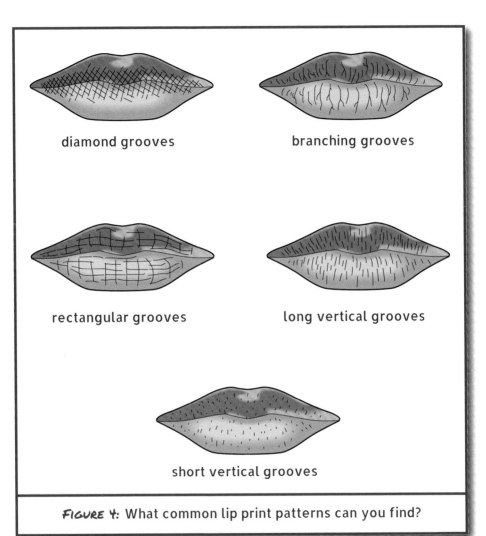

diamond grooves

branching grooves

rectangular grooves

long vertical grooves

short vertical grooves

FIGURE 4: What common lip print patterns can you find?

4. Ask a group of people whose lip prints you have recorded to choose one person from the group to leave a lip print on a glass or tissue. From your lip print records, can you determine who left the lip print?

Casting Footprints

Footprints of bare feet are seldom found at crime scenes. However, tracks left by shoes or tires are quite common and can be photographed. It is also possible to make casts of tracks found in soft soil by pouring plaster of Paris into the track. After the cast dries, it can be removed and carried to a laboratory.

YOU WILL NEED

- AN ADULT
- WHITE PAPER
- SHOE TRACK OR TIRE TRACK IN SOFT SOIL
- SCISSORS
- THIN CARDBOARD
- PAPER CLIPS
- LARGE PAPER CUP
- PLASTER OF PARIS
- WATER
- STICK
- CANDLES
- MATCHES

A cast or photograph of a shoe print or tire print can be compared with a suspect's shoes or car.

1. Place some white paper sheets near the door where family members or classmates enter your home or classroom. If you obtain any clear tracks, can you locate the shoes that made them?

2. Find a shoe track or tire track in soft soil. To make a cast of

the track, first cut a strip of thin cardboard about 4 cm (1.5 in) wide and a few centimeters longer than is needed to surround the track. Use several paper clips to hold the ends of the strip together in a loop. Place the cardboard collar around the track as shown in Figure 5.

3. Fill a large paper cup halfway with plaster of Paris. Slowly

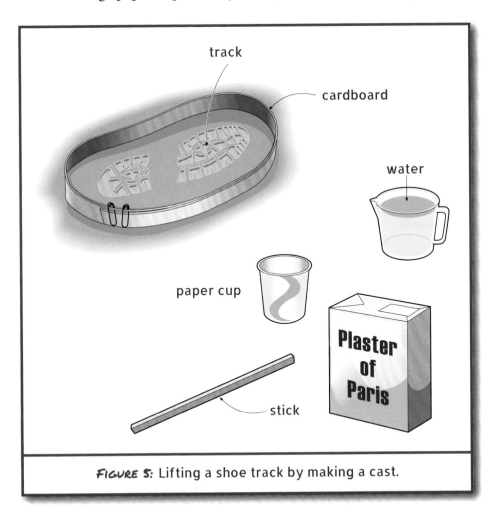

FIGURE 5: Lifting a shoe track by making a cast.

add water to the plaster as you stir with a stick. It is important that the plaster be the right consistency. It should not be too thick or too watery. It has the right consistency when it will pour slowly out of the cup like thick oatmeal. You can adjust the consistency by adding a little water or a little plaster and stirring some more. Before pouring the plaster into the track, tap the cup on the ground a few times to free any air bubbles trapped inside the plaster.

4. Add the wet plaster until it completely fills the track. Wait about half an hour for the plaster to harden. Then remove the cast. Turn it over, wash off the dirt or mud, and you should see a preserved copy of the track.

Now for the detective work. What made the track?

You can even make casts of tracks found in snow. If melted wax (paraffin) is added slowly to the track, it hardens instantly. Layer after layer of wax can be added to make a cast. This can be done with a burning candle.

5. Ask an adult to hold a burning candle on its side. The melted wax will drip onto the track and slowly a cast of the track can be made.

Studying Voiceprints

Voiceprints are made using a sound spectrograph that converts speech sounds into a visual display called a voiceprint. Forensic scientists compare the voiceprint of a suspect with one made from a recording collected as evidence.

YOU WILL NEED

- SMALL MIRROR [ABOUT 2.5 CM (1 IN) SQUARE]
- INFLATED BALLOON
- DOUBLE-SIDED STICKY TAPE
- A FRIEND
- DARK ROOM
- FLASHLIGHT OR PENCIL LASER

1. You can use a mechanical analogy to see something similar to a voiceprint. Attach a small mirror (2.5 cm x 2.5 cm, or 1 inch x 1 inch) to an inflated balloon using double-sided sticky tape.

2. Have one person hold the balloon gently. In a dark room, have a second person shine a flashlight or a pencil laser onto the mirror. (If you use a pencil laser, **do not shine it into anyone's eyes.**) The reflected light from the mirror will appear on a wall or ceiling as shown in Figure 6.

3. Have the person holding the balloon speak or sing some words

at the balloon. Watch the reflected beam on the wall. Notice how it moves in response to the sounds reaching the balloon.

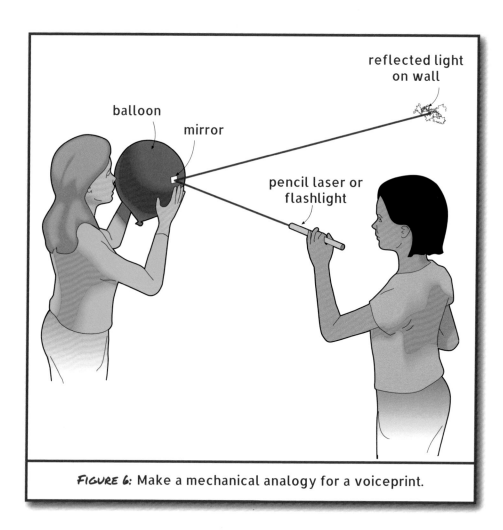

FIGURE 6: Make a mechanical analogy for a voiceprint.

CHAPTER 4

Solving Crimes Using the Physical Sciences

Both chemistry and physics are used in forensic science. These branches of science provide the information to uncover clues from a crime scene or on a body. For example, as early as 1840 a chemical test, known as the Marsh test, was used to confirm the presence of arsenic in a victim. [Arsenic is actually a brittle, steel-gray metal. The poisonous substance often referred to as arsenic is really arsenic trioxide (As_2O_3), a white powder.] The test was developed by James Marsh in 1830. Marsh discovered that tissue containing arsenic (As_2O_3) produces arsine gas (AsH_3) when added to acid and zinc. Arsine, when heated, breaks into arsenic and hydrogen. Marsh found that a cold porcelain dish held above the hot gas becomes coated with a black deposit of arsenic.

The Marsh test was first used as evidence during the trial of Marie Lafarge. Police believed that Marie had poisoned her husband with arsenic. A family maid claimed she had seen Marie putting white powder in her husband's food. The maid gave some of the powder to the police who arrested Marie.

At the trial, the prosecution learned of the Marsh test from a famous toxicologist, Mathieu Joseph Bonaventure Orfila. Orfila used the test on tissue taken from the victim, Charles Lafarge. He found traces of arsenic in Lafarge's stomach, liver, heart, brain, and intestines. Based on the Marsh test evidence, Marie was found guilty and sentenced to life in prison.

Today, arsenic poisoning, which some believe led to the death of Napoleon Bonaparte, is quite rare. However, in 1998, a Japanese couple, Masumi and Kenji Hayashi, were arrested for attempting to poison a friend who had become very sick after dining with the Hayashis. The friend spent four months in the hospital and finally recovered from what was diagnosed as arsenic poisoning. Police investigated and found that the Hayashis had taken out life insurance policies on the man, without his knowledge, that totaled more than a million dollars.

The next experiment will help you to develop a sense of how forensic chemists carry out tests to identify unknown substances found at a crime scene.

What Are These White Solids?

1. In separate plastic cups, put a tablespoonful of the following powders: cornstarch, white flour, sugar, salt, and baking soda. Label each cup with the substance it contains. You will carry out tests on each substance.

2. Prepare a table in your notebook like Table 2. Record all your observations in your notebook table.

YOU WILL NEED

- AN ADULT
- TABLESPOON
- PLASTIC CUPS
- CORNSTARCH
- WHITE FLOUR
- SUGAR
- SALT
- BAKING SODA
- NOTEBOOK
- SET OF MEASURING SPOONS
- PEN OR PENCIL
- MAGNIFIER
- DRINKING GLASSES
- WATER

- WOODEN COFFEE STIRRERS
- PLASTIC MEDICINE CUPS OR VIALS
- TINCTURE OF IODINE (OBTAIN FROM A PHARMACY)
- DROPPER
- FRYING PAN
- STOVE
- VINEGAR
- 6.3-VOLT FLASHLIGHT BULB
- BULB HOLDER
- 6-VOLT BATTERY
- ELECTRIC WIRE
- 2 NAILS

APPEARANCE TEST

Can you identify any of these substances by their appearance (look)? Does examining them with a magnifying lens help you identify them?

FEEL TEST

Rub a small amount of each white substance between your fingers. Does the way they feel help you identify any of them?

SOLUBILITY TEST

Add ¼ teaspoon of cornstarch to half a glass of water. Stir the

Substance	Look	Feel	Solubility in Water	Reaction with Iodine	Reaction when Heated	Reaction with Vinegar	Conducts Electricity?
Cornstarch							
Flour							
Sugar							
Salt							
Baking soda							
Unknown							

TABLE 2: Test Results of Five White Substances and an Unknown

mixture. Does the starch dissolve? Dump the mixture down the drain and flush with water. Record your results in the table you prepared.

Repeat the test for each white solid. Which substances dissolve (are soluble) in water? Which are insoluble (do not dissolve)?

IODINE TEST

Place ¼ teaspoon of each white substance in separate plastic medicine cups or vials that you have labeled. (Do not use paper cups or plates.) **Under adult supervision**, prepare a test solution of iodine by adding two drops of tincture of iodine to 50 drops of water in a separate plastic container. (**Iodine is poisonous. Do not get it near your mouth!**) Using a dropper, add several drops of the iodine solution to each of the white solids. Which solids turn dark blue when iodine is added? Be sure to record your results.

HEAT TEST

Put ½ teaspoon of each solid on the bottom of a frying pan. Make a labeled diagram showing the position of each solid in the pan. In this way you will be able to remember where each solid is.

Place the pan on a stove. **Ask an adult to slowly heat the pan.** Do any of the solids melt when heated? Do any change into something else? Which powders might you identify by heating? Let the pan cool while you do additional tests. After it has cooled, it should be washed.

VINEGAR TEST

Put ¼ teaspoon of each powder in separate plastic medicine cups or vials. Add a few drops of vinegar to each solid. What happens in each case? Can you identify any of the solids by adding vinegar?

CONDUCTIVITY TEST

Put ½ teaspoon of each powder in separate plastic medicine cups or vials. Label each cup or vial so you know which solid is in it. Add 20 mL (or 4 teaspoons) of water to each solid and stir. Use the apparatus shown in Figure 7 to see which, if any, of the solids mixed with water will conduct electricity.

The circuit shown in Figure 7 has a 6.3-volt flashlight bulb in a bulb holder. One side of the bulb is connected to one terminal of a 6-volt dry cell battery. The other side of the bulb is connected to a nail. A second nail is connected to the other terminal of the battery. Will a mixture of any of the solids with water conduct electricity?

To find out, put the nails in one of the solid-water mixtures. **Be sure the nails do not touch each other.** (The nails, if touching, will conduct electricity, but the test is to see if any of the solids dissolved in water will conduct electricity.) If the bulb lights, you know the dissolved solid conducts electricity.

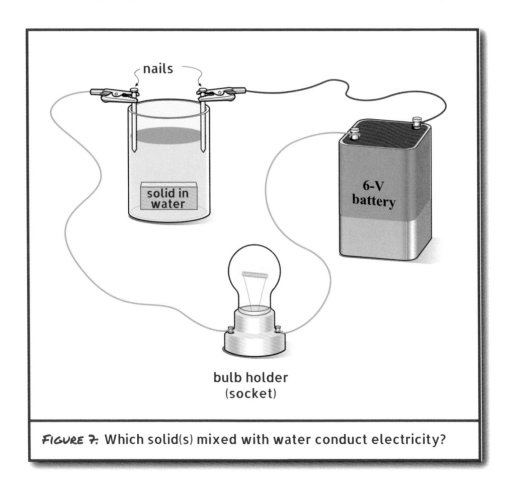

nails

solid in
water

6-V
battery

bulb holder
(socket)

FIGURE 7: Which solid(s) mixed with water conduct electricity?

Rinse the nails with water after testing each solid-water mixture.

What do you find? Do any of the solids conduct electricity when mixed with water? Can the conductivity test help you identify any of the white solids?

TESTING AN UNKNOWN

While you are not looking, have someone select one of the solids and give it to you. Carry out the tests you have used. Can you identify the solid?

Glass as Evidence

Glass, found at the scene of a crime, is often valuable evidence. It is common for burglars to break a window in order to enter a building. When they do this, even though they push the glass inward, some of the glass particles always fly back at them and become trapped in their clothes. Glass detected on a suspect's clothes can be tested to see if it came from the scene of a crime.

YOU WILL NEED

• A CHILD'S UNASSEMBLED JIGSAW PUZZLE WITH RELATIVELY FEW PIECES

DO THE PIECES MATCH?

In a hit-and-run accident, glass from a car's headlight is often found at the scene of the collision or on the victim's body. If police find a car with a broken headlight, they can often use glass as evidence in several ways. Sometimes pieces of glass at a crime scene can be matched with pieces collected from a suspect. To see how this works, remove some of the pieces from a child's unassembled jigsaw puzzle. Put the remaining pieces together as best you can.

Assume the pieces you tried to put together are pieces of glass collected at the scene of a hit-and-run accident. Assume the pieces you removed are pieces found on the broken headlight of a suspect's car.

Do the pieces of "glass" you collected at the crime scene fit together with the pieces of "glass" found on the suspect's broken headlight? Would the fit of the pieces convince a jury that the suspect is guilty?

Is the Density the Same?

Scientists might also measure the density of the glass collected at a crime scene. Density is the mass of a substance per volume. To measure the density of glass evidence, you could weigh the glass and also measure the volume of the glass. The density of the glass would be its mass divided by its volume. If its mass were 25 grams (g) and its volume 10 cubic centimeters (cm^3), its density would be 2.5 g/cm^3 because 25 g/10 cm^3 = 2.5 g/cm^3.

Usually, the pieces of glass are quite small; consequently, the scientists have to use very sensitive instruments. A match in densities between glass from the suspect and glass from the crime scene proves the suspect *could have* been there. If the densities do not match, then the glass found on the suspect did not come from the scene of the crime.

Density and Glass Evidence

Forensic scientists use expensive equipment to measure the density of the small pieces of glass commonly found at a crime scene. You can make density measurements using much larger pieces of glass and less expensive apparatus.

YOU WILL NEED

- SMALL GLASS JARS
- A METRIC BALANCE
- METRIC MEASURING CUP
- WATER
- NOTEBOOK
- PEN OR PENCIL
- SMALL PLASTIC JAR OR ANOTHER GLASS OBJECT
- EGG
- LARGE JAR
- KOSHER SALT
- COFFEE STIRRER
- DROPPER

1. Find an empty glass jar. Remove the cap or lid and then weigh the jar on a balance. What is the mass of the jar in grams?

2. To find the volume of the jar, add water to a metric measuring cup. Fill it to a level that will cover the jar when you submerge the jar in the measuring cup.

3. Record the volume, in cubic centimeters (cm³), of the water in the measuring cup. [It does not matter if the measuring cup measures volume in milliliters (mL) because a cubic centimeter (cm^3) and a milliliter (mL) are equal in volume.]

4. Completely submerge the jar in the measuring cup. Measure the water level after the jar has been submerged. What is the volume now? How can you find the volume of the glass?

5. Knowing the volume and mass of the glass in the jar, you can find the density of the glass. Simply divide its mass in grams by its volume in cubic centimeters. What is the density of the glass jar?

6. Repeat the experiment. This time find the density of a small plastic jar or a different glass object. How do the two densities compare?

The density of glass fragments at a crime lab is often found using a familiar principle. Solids more dense than a liquid will sink in that liquid, while substances less dense than the liquid will float. An object with the same density as the liquid will remain suspended in the liquid and neither sink nor float.

Forensic scientists find the density of glass particles by putting them in a mixture of two liquids. One liquid has a density slightly greater than the density range for different kinds of glass. A second liquid has a density slightly less than the density range for different kinds of glass. The mix of the two liquids is adjusted until the glass neither sinks nor floats but remains suspended. The density of the glass then matches the density of the liquid mixture, which can be easily determined to within 0.0003 g (3 ten-thousandths of a gram) per cubic centimeter.

7. You can adjust the density of a liquid to match the density of something else. Put a fresh egg in a large jar of water. As you can see, the egg sinks. What does this tell you about the density of an egg?

8. Now add a small amount of kosher salt to the jar and stir until the salt dissolves. Continue to add salt and stir until the egg just barely floats. What can you say about the density of the liquid now?

9. Next, patiently add water drop by drop with stirring until the egg remains suspended in the water—until it neither sinks nor floats. How does the density of the egg compare with the density of the liquid now?

If glass particles from a suspect and a crime scene have different densities, they could not have come from the same source. If, however, their densities are the same, they *may* have come from the same source.

Ideas for your Science Fair

- Measure the density of the egg by finding the density of the liquid in which it remains suspended.
- Show how forensic scientists might use color, shape, scratches, and designs on glass as evidence.

Refractivity and Glass Evidence

Glass evidence is also tested by measuring the refractivity of the glass: that is, how much the glass bends light. Light bends when it passes from one transparent substance, such as air, into another, such as water or glass.

1. To see that this is true, pour a cup of water into a clear jar. Add 10–12 drops of milk to the water and stir. Place the jar on a sheet of white paper resting on a table in a dark room. Hold a comb in front of the jar. Shine a flashlight through the comb into the jar as shown in Figure 8a. What happens to the narrow beams (rays) of light as they enter and leave the jar?

2. Notice how the light is bent and brought together by the cylindrical shape of the water. A glass lens bends light in a similar way.

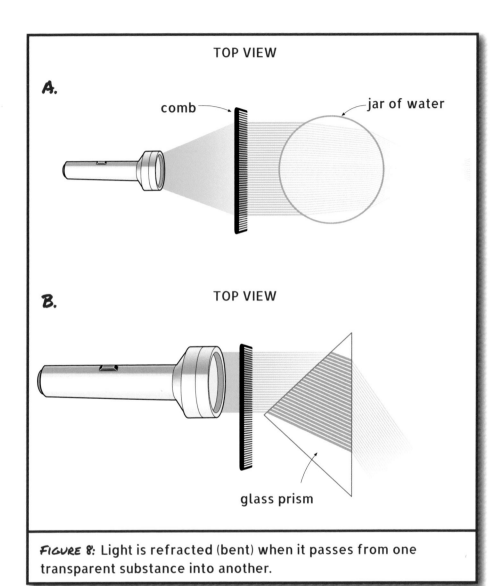

TOP VIEW

A.

comb

jar of water

B.

TOP VIEW

glass prism

FIGURE 8: Light is refracted (bent) when it passes from one transparent substance into another.

3. To see that glass bends light, use the flashlight and comb to shine rays of light into a glass prism as shown in Figure 8b. You may see that the colors that are combined in white light are refracted slightly differently. The result is a spectrum of colors. Which color bends the most? The least?

Some kinds of glass refract light more than others. By measuring the refractivity of glass collected at a crime scene, forensic scientists can often determine whether the glass came from a window, headlight, glass jar, paperweight, or some other source.

The FBI has a database of refractivities for many types of glass. That database can be used to see how common a glass with a certain refractivity is. Suppose the refractivity of a piece of glass from a hit-and-run crime scene matches the refractivity of a suspect's broken headlight. If the probability of the match is one in a thousand, the evidence could convince a jury that the suspect is guilty.

Refractivity by Immersion and Glass Evidence

Usually, glass collected at a crime scene consists of pieces that are too small to be used to bend a narrow beam of light. Forensic scientists often use a less direct way to measure the refractivity of glass evidence. They use different transparent liquids that refract

YOU WILL NEED

- TRANSPARENT PLASTIC TAPE
- LIGHT-COLORED COOKING OIL
- CLEAN GLASS OR BEAKER
- GLASS STIRRING ROD (OPTIONAL)

light by different amounts. If a piece of glass evidence is put in a liquid that refracts light the same amount as the glass, the glass disappears! Light going through the liquid "sees" the glass and the liquid as the same substance. The light is not bent or reflected as it goes through the glass, so it is invisible while in the liquid.

Forensic scientists usually measure the refractivity of glass fragments by putting them in a clear silicone oil, which is then heated or cooled. The refractivity of the oil changes with temperature. When the glass particles disappear, their refractivity matches the oil's, which has been carefully measured at different temperatures. Modern crime labs use an instrument that performs the analysis automatically using a computer. A human who carries out the experiment then confirms the refractivity.

If glass from the scene of a crime and glass found on a suspect are suspended in a clear silicone oil and both disappear at the same temperature, then the investigator knows that the two glass samples refract light in the same way. If their densities also match, then the two samples may well have come from the same source. On the other hand, if either the density or the refractive properties of the glass do not match, then the glass found on the suspect did not come from the scene of the crime.

1. To see how the refractivity of two materials can be compared, find some transparent plastic tape. Be careful. Some plastic tape is not clear. The refractivity of clear tape is almost the same as clear or light-colored cooking oil. Pour some clear cooking oil into a clean glass or beaker. Then dip one end of the transparent plastic tape into the oil. What happens to the visibility of the end of the tape submerged in the oil?

2. If you have a glass stirring rod or can borrow one from your

school's science lab, put the stirring rod in the clear cooking oil. The oil bends light the same (or nearly the same) amount as the glass rod. The bottom of the stirring rod will disappear. If the glass and liquid do not have *exactly* the same refractivity, you will be able to see the submerged glass rod when you look closely.

IDEAS FOR YOUR SCIENCE FAIR

- Investigate the meaning of refractive index. Then measure the refractive indexes of various solids and liquids such as water, alcohol, mineral oil, glass, plastic, and other materials.
- Is the refractive index of a substance proportional to its density?

CHAPTER 5

Solving Crimes Using the Biological Sciences

The biological sciences can also be useful in solving crimes. Bones, teeth, blood, DNA, body temperature, insects—even microorganisms—are used by forensic scientists to solve crimes. As a result, criminalists often turn to dentists, physical anthropologists, bacteriologists, microbiologists, biochemists, physicians, and other professionals trained in the many biological specialties to help them investigate crimes.

In this chapter you will learn how scientists study biological evidence, including hair and fibers. You will test some of the identification techniques and see how biology plays a part in solving crimes.

EXPERIMENT 5.1
Teeth Impressions

1. Using scissors, cut square pieces about 8 cm (3 in) on a side from Styrofoam cups. Put two pieces, one on top of the other, into your mouth. Bite down firmly on the Styrofoam pieces. Remove them from your mouth.

2. Label the top piece "Upper" and the lower piece "Lower." Compare the impressions. How can you distinguish the impressions made by the upper teeth from those made by the lower teeth?

3. Collect teeth impressions from family members, friends, and classmates. Label the top and bottom teeth marks and the name of the person who made the impressions.

4. In your absence, ask that one of your friends or a family member whose teeth impressions you have on file take a bite out of a large piece of cheese or hard chocolate. Using the

Styrofoam impressions you have collected, can you identify the person who bit the cheese or chocolate?

Teeth impressions have been used to solve a number of real crimes. In one case, detectives found a wad of chewing gum with teeth marks at the scene of a murder. A forensic dentist made casts of the impressions by applying silicone to the hardened gum. The teeth that chewed the gum did not match the teeth of the victim; however, they did match impressions taken from a suspect. Forensic scientists were able to collect enough saliva from the gum to determine the blood type of the chewer. It was type AB blood, which is found in only 4 percent of the population, but it matched the suspect's blood type. Facing both pieces of evidence, the suspect confessed to the crime.

Studying Bones to Solve Crimes

Bones hold clues. Physical anthropologists, scientists who examine the fossilized bones of our ancient human ancestors, can use those clues to solve crimes. The FBI often brings skeletal remains of a victim to a physical anthropologist with a list of

YOU WILL NEED

- SEVERAL ADULTS
- PENCIL AND PAPER
- A WALL
- TAPE
- TAPE MEASURE OR YARDSTICK
- CALCULATOR (OPTIONAL)

questions. Are the bones human? If so, how old was the victim? Was the victim male or female? Caucasian, Hispanic, African American, Asian, or American Indian? Tall or short? Was he or she muscular? Did the person have any diseases or distinctive features? Were the bones charred, indicating that the victim was burned? Were any bones broken?

The fused bones of the pelvis are useful in determining whether the skeletal remains are those of a male or a female. A human female's pelvis is wider and more shallow than a male's. If the skeleton's teeth are intact, dental records can often be used to identify the skeletal remains. Height is easy to determine from a complete skeleton, but anthropologists have found ways to estimate height from partial skeletons by using mathematics. You can see how that works by doing an experiment.

1. Ask several adults to let you measure their height, foot, forearm, arms, and hands. (Record all your measurements in a chart like the one shown in Table 3.)

2. Ask each person you measure to remove his or her shoes and stand against a door. Place a level ruler on top of the

Name:				
Height:				
Length of foot:				
Length from elbow to wrist:				
Length of cubit:				
Length of span:				
Distance between fingertips of outstretched arms:				

TABLE 3: Body Measurements

person's head. Use a pencil to mark the end of the ruler on a piece of tape on the door. Later, you can use a tape measure or yardstick to measure the person's height in centimeters or inches.

3. Ask the person to put the heel of one foot firmly against the wall. Measure the length of his or her foot from the wall to the tip of the big toe.

4. Measure the following lengths: from the tip of the elbow to the wrist; the cubit (distance from elbow to tip of middle finger); span (distance between tips of thumb and little finger of outstretched hand); between the fingertips of the arms when both are outstretched to the side.

5. For each person you measure, find the ratio of height to length of foot. For example, if a man is 180 cm tall and his foot is 27 cm long, then the ratio of height to foot length is

$$\frac{180 \text{ cm}}{27 \text{ cm}}$$

6. Also, for each person find the following ratios: height to the length of elbow to wrist; height to cubit; height to span; and height to distance between fingertips of outstretched arms.

Which of the ratios are very nearly the same for everyone you measured? From these ratios for different people, how do you think anthropologists make good estimates of height when only some of the bones of a victim are found?

PHYSICAL ANTHROPOLOGISTS AT WORK

In 1948, Josef Mengele, a Nazi responsible for the deaths of 400,000 people at the Auschwitz concentration camp in World War II, fled to South America.

Nearly forty years later, in 1985, authorities in Brazil were led to the grave of Wolfgang Gerhard. Mr. and Mrs. Wolfram, a German couple living in Brazil, told them that the grave really contained the remains of Josef Mengele, the notorious Nazi who had drowned several years earlier.

Anthropologists examined the skeletal remains. The narrow pelvis indicated the deceased was male. The bones on the right arm were longer than those on the left, indicating that the man had been right-handed. Bone lengths, like the ones you measured, indicated he had been 173.5 cm (68.3 inches) tall—very close to Mengele's height as recorded in his military records. The teeth matched Mengele's dental records, and images from photographs of Mengele superimposed onto photographs of the exhumed skull matched perfectly. Later, DNA obtained from the skeletal remains was compared with

DNA from members of Mengele's family who were still living in Germany. The DNA results confirmed that Wolfgang Gerhard had really been Josef Mengele, the "Angel of Death," who was never brought to justice.

Microbe Clues and Drowning

The discovery of a drowning victim often raises a question for forensic scientists. Was the drowning accidental or was it murder? In some cases, evidence suggests that the victim was murdered before being dumped in water and that the cause of death was not drowning.

YOU WILL NEED

- AN ADULT
- JARS WITH LIDS
- PONDS OR LAKES
- MICROSCOPE
- PAPER AND PENCIL

In most cases of drowning, suffocation results when water fills the lungs, but "dry drowning" occurs in about one fifth of drowning victims. In dry drowning, a reflex reaction contracts the muscles around the larynx (voice box) when water hits it. This keeps water from going into the lungs and causes another reflex that stops the heart. Victims of dry drowning are found with very little water in their lungs.

In "wet drowning," which is more common, the lungs fill with water. This prevents oxygen from reaching the blood, and the victim soon loses consciousness. A coroner examining a wet drowning victim will find soggy lungs, water in the stomach, and diluted blood in the left side of the heart. If the victim was dead before being thrown into water, the blood in the heart will not be diluted.

Involuntary breathing by a drowning victim pulls water into the lungs and stomach and from there to the blood and the various organs of the body. Such a victim's body will contain a variety of diatoms (microscopic plants) that will be found in the body's tissues during an autopsy. A corpse thrown into

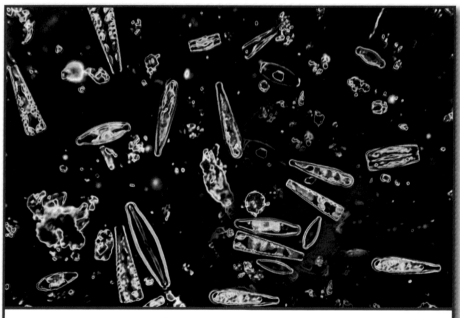

FIGURE 9: Diatoms are single-celled algae. They live in saltwater and freshwater. They vary in appearance, depending on where they live.

water will have diatoms in the lungs but not in other body tissues. Because diatom species from various locations differ, a careful analysis of diatoms in a drowning victim may also reveal where the drowning occurred.

1. **Have an adult** help you collect some water in a jar from a pond or lake. Put a lid on the jar and bring it home or to your school.

2. Examine drops of the water through a microscope. If you have never used a microscope, ask a science teacher or someone familiar with the instrument to help you. Can you find diatoms like those shown in Figure 9? Make drawings of some of the diatoms you see.

3. **Have an adult** help you collect water samples from several different locations. Do the diatoms from different locations differ? Could you use the diatoms to identify the source of the water?

Decomposition Clues

Human tissue, like all organic (living) matter, decomposes (breaks down). The rate of decay depends on temperature, weather, soil conditions, insects, and other factors. Forensic scientists can estimate the approximate date of a victim's death from the degree to which a corpse has decomposed. You can do an experiment to see how different kinds of matter decompose over time.

1. Soil contains fungi and bacteria that cause the breakdown of many kinds of tissue. To see what kinds of tissue decompose in soil, collect some items such as

YOU WILL NEED

- APPLE CORE, BANANA PEEL, COOKIE, LETTUCE LEAVES, A COOKED CHICKEN BONE WITH SOME MEAT ATTACHED, PAPER, PLASTIC BAG, ALUMINUM CAN, STYROFOAM CUP, OTHER THINGS YOU MIGHT THROW AWAY
- SHOVEL
- WOODEN COFFEE STIRRERS
- PEN
- GLOVES
- LARGE STONE OR CONCRETE BLOCK
- BREAD, TOMATO, CRACKERS
- CLEAR PLASTIC BOXES WITH CLEAR LIDS OR COVERS
- WATER
- DRY COOKIE, DRY CEREAL, DOG BISCUIT

an apple core, a banana peel, a cookie, lettuce leaves, a cooked chicken bone with some meat attached, a piece of paper, a plastic bag, an aluminum can, a Styrofoam cup, and other things you might throw away.

2. Dig a small hole in the ground near your house, school, or a park for each of the items you collected. Choose an out-of-the-way place that is not likely to be disturbed. Be sure to obtain permission before you dig any holes.

3. Use a labeled wooden coffee stirrer to identify the location of each item after you bury it. All food items should be placed in the same hole and covered with the dug soil. Place a large stone or concrete block on top of the buried items so that animals cannot reach them.

4. Every month or two carefully uncover the items you buried. Wear gloves when you do this. Which items decompose within a few months? Which items seem not to decay at all? Of the items that decay, how does temperature affect the rate of decay? Do they decay faster in summer or in winter?

5. You can watch things decay. Place some pieces of bread, tomato, and crackers in separate clear plastic boxes that have lids. Choose boxes that can be thrown away when the

experiment is finished. Add a few drops of water to each item and put the lid back on each box.

6. Put the boxes in a moderately cool place (12–18°C or 55–65°F) where you can watch them. After a few days, you will probably see mold, bacterial colonies, and various other fungi growing on the food. Often the mold will produce tiny black spores that give the food a dark appearance. Molds reproduce by spores. Each spore can grow into a new mold and produce its own spores.

7. Continue watching. Can you see the food gradually disappear as it is consumed by the decomposers? **Do not open the boxes when you put them in the garbage! You should not breathe in mold spores or get them in your mouth!**

8. Is moisture needed for things to decompose? To find out, place a few dry foods—a dry cookie, some dry cereal, a piece of dog biscuit—in each of two plastic containers. To one container add enough water to dampen each food item. Add no water to the second. Put clear covers on both boxes and put them in a place where the temperature is moderately cool (12–18°C or 55–65°F). Watch them over the course of several months. What do you conclude? **Do not open the boxes when you put**

them in the garbage! You should not breathe in mold spores or get them in your mouth!

IDEAS FOR YOUR SCIENCE FAIR

- How can food be kept from decomposing? Investigate the various methods used to preserve food. How does each method prevent food from decaying?
- Will preserved foods ever decay?

Temperature and Time of Death

A medical examiner or coroner will try to determine the time of death of a victim connected to a possible crime. One way to do this is to measure the temperature of the body. After death, the body no longer generates heat and so it cools. Doing an experiment will help you see how temperature can be used to estimate time of death.

YOU WILL NEED

- AN ADULT
- CUP OF HOT COFFEE
- THERMOMETER WITH A RANGE OF –10°C–110°C OR 0°F–220°F
- CLOCK OR WATCH
- PENCIL AND PAPER
- GRAPH PAPER
- BASIN
- ICE
- TAP WATER, HOT AND COLD
- METRIC MEASURING CUP OR GRADUATED CYLINDER
- METAL CAN
- GLASS JAR
- STYROFOAM CUP

1. **Ask an adult** to fill a cup with hot coffee. Place an alcohol-based thermometer in the cup. Record the temperature of the hot coffee. Record the time as zero. Then, in a chart like the one on the next page, record the temperature at two-minute intervals until the temperature stops changing.

2. Using graph paper, plot a graph of temperature on the vertical

axis against time on the horizontal axis. When does the coffee cool fastest? Slowest?

3. You can use your graph to determine how long a cup of coffee has been cooling. **Ask the adult** to pour another cup of hot coffee a few minutes after you leave the room. Then, have the adult, after waiting a few minutes more, ask you back into the room.

4. Measure the temperature of the coffee. Use your graph to estimate how much time has passed since the coffee was poured.

5. Does the temperature of the surroundings affect the rate at which a cup of hot coffee cools? Design and carry out an experiment to find out.

Temperature (degrees)	Time (min)
0	
2	
4	
. . .	

How would the rate of cooling of a body lying in a snow bank compare with that of a body lying in a warm room?

The body of an obese person or a person dressed in heavy clothing is surrounded by insulating material. How might these factors affect the rate of cooling?

6. To find out, fill a basin with a mixture of ice and cold tap water to a depth of about 5 cm (2 in).

7. Pour 150 mL (about ⅝ cup) of hot tap water into a metal can. Measure the temperature of the hot water.

8. Put the can of hot water into the ice water. Measure the temperature of the water in the can every minute until it reaches 10°C (50°F). Record the temperatures and times in a table.

9. Repeat the experiment using a glass jar with the same amount of hot water at the same initial temperature. Do the experiment a third time using a Styrofoam cup.

10. Plot temperature versus time, as before, on graph paper. You can plot the results of all three experiments on the same graph. In which container does the water cool fastest? Slowest?

Styrofoam is a good insulator. How does insulation (fat) affect the rate that a body cools? How would a medical examiner or coroner take obesity into account when trying to establish time of death by body temperature?

IDEAS FOR YOUR SCIENCE FAIR

- Design and conduct experiments to compare the insulating quality of different materials such as Styrofoam, paper, fiberglass, air, wood, and others.
- What is meant by the R-value of an insulating material? Design and conduct experiments to measure the R-value of various insulating materials.

DNA EVIDENCE

DNA (deoxyribonucleic acid) is contained in the chromosomes that are passed from one generation to the next. Chromosomes are located in the nucleus of most body cells. As a result, DNA can be obtained from nearly all of the body cells left at the scene of a crime.

DNA is almost as unique as fingerprints. Only identical twins have the same DNA. Because DNA is so unique, it is used extensively by forensic scientists even though DNA testing is expensive.

Forensic DNA typing involves obtaining two samples: one, such as blood, semen, saliva, or skin tissue from the crime scene; and a second blood or saliva sample from a suspect. By comparing the DNA from the two samples, scientists can determine the likelihood that the samples came from the same individual.

The testing requires thousands of DNA molecules. However, DNA samples are often limited to a sample of dried saliva left on a cigarette. DNA polymerases to the rescue! These enzymes make billions of copies of the original DNA in the laboratory. As few as 50 molecules of DNA from a crime scene can be copied repeatedly to prepare a billion times as much DNA for testing.

Only very small samples are needed because of a technique known as the polymerase chain reaction (PCR). Using PCR, DNA extracted from a sample is heated to about 95°C (203°F) together with DNA nucleotides. DNA nucleotides are a sugar molecule and a phosphate molecule hooked to one of four nitrogen-containing bases: thymine (T), adenine (A), guanine (G), or cytosine (C). They join in one way only: T with A, and G with C. Also in the mix are DNA "primer" sequences and polymerase. Polymerase is an enzyme that promotes the copying of the DNA. The primers are short artificial sequences of DNA that cause copying to start at the right places.

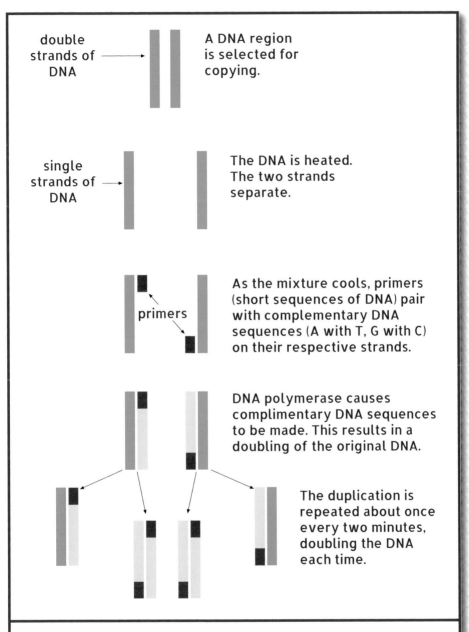

double strands of DNA → A DNA region is selected for copying.

single strands of DNA → The DNA is heated. The two strands separate.

primers → As the mixture cools, primers (short sequences of DNA) pair with complementary DNA sequences (A with T, G with C) on their respective strands.

DNA polymerase causes complimentary DNA sequences to be made. This results in a doubling of the original DNA.

The duplication is repeated about once every two minutes, doubling the DNA each time.

FIGURE 10: PCR can quickly increase a small sample of DNA by billions of times.

Heating separates the two strands of DNA that form the double helix. As the separated strands cool, the primers attach to the separated strands. The primers send "signals" to the DNA polymerase enzymes "saying," "Start adding nucleotides here." (See Figure 10.) Starting at the primers, the polymerase links nucleotides to the DNA strands always, remember, T with A and G with C. This results in two double-stranded lengths of DNA identical to the original double strand. Consequently, the original DNA sample has been doubled.

Since this doubling process occurs approximately every two minutes, billions of copies of the original DNA sample have been made after 90 minutes.

By selecting primers, the sequence of a DNA strand that is copied can be limited to a small part of the total genome (all the DNA in a cell). The regions that are selected are ones where individual humans are known to differ.

Human chromosomes have short segments of DNA where nucleotides are repeated three to fifty times. These are called *short tandem repeats*, or *STRs* for short. For example, a segment might have an STR such as TCAT. At a given location in the genome, one person will have a certain number of STRs while someone else will have a different number of STRs. For example, individual A may have TCAT TCAT TCAT TCAT TCAT, while individual B may have TCAT TCAT TCAT. The likelihood that two unrelated people will have the same number of tandem repeats at one location in the genome is small (5–20 percent). But in forensic DNA typing, 13 such locations are examined. If the STR patterns at 13 locations of two DNA samples (one from a suspect and one from a crime scene) are identical, there is an overwhelming probability that the two samples are from the same individual. For example, even if the probability of identical tandem repeats at all 13 sites is 20 percent (0.2), the possibility that samples from two individuals will be identical is 0.2 x 0.2 x 0.2 x 0.2 x 0.2 x 0.2 x 0.2 x 0.2 x 0.2 x 0.2 x 0.2 x 0.2 x 0.2 = 0.00000000082, or just less than one in a billion.

During the PCR process, the DNA samples are mixed with fluorescent dyes before the material is placed in a special gel. An electric field applied to the gel separates the DNA pieces according to size. A laser connected to a computer "looks" at the DNA and displays the results as peaks that are compared with peaks of all the possible variations at each of the 13 locations that are examined. If the peaks from the two samples

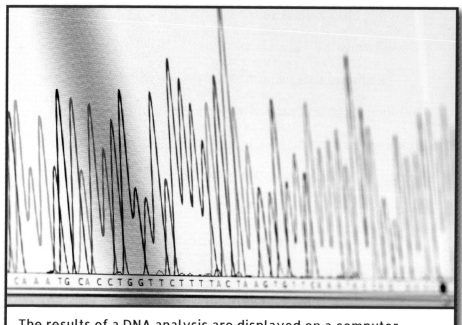

CA A A TG CA C CTGGT TCTTT TACTA AG

The results of a DNA analysis are displayed on a computer screen.

match, the evidence is overwhelming that they came from the same person.

All states now require that persons convicted of a violent crime provide a DNA sample, which is stored for future reference. The FBI has a national database of the DNA.

DNA Evidence

Before the present method of
DNA analysis was developed,
DNA from the two samples
(crime scene and suspect) were

placed side by side in a gel and subjected to electrophoresis
(an electric current passed through the gel). Because DNA
surfaces are slightly negative, the DNA molecules moved
toward the positively charged electrode. But the lighter
molecules moved faster than the heavier ones, so the DNA in
both samples separated into bands.

Once the electrophoresis was completed, the separated
DNA fragments were transferred to a nylon membrane in
much the same way that ink can be transferred to a blotter.
Next, radioactive DNA probes (pieces of DNA that had been
exposed to radiation) became bound to specific fragments
of the DNA, called targets. Then x-ray film was placed over
the nylon for several days. When the film was developed, the

"DNA" from suspects with initials shown

JAK

DBI

ACZ

LDL

AME

"DNA" found at a crime scene

Figure 11: "DNA profiles" from a crime scene and from five suspects.

bands, which had been made radioactive by the probes, could be seen on the x-ray film.

By comparing the patterns of bands, an investigator can determine whether two DNA samples might have come from the same person.

The parallel bands obtained in these earlier DNA tests resembled the bar codes used in identifying and pricing items in a supermarket.

In Figure 11, bar codes are used to represent DNA patterns. Assume one pattern came from DNA collected at a crime scene. Assume, too, that five suspects have been arrested and their DNA has been analyzed producing the five patterns shown in Figure 11. Were any of the five suspects at the scene of the crime? (Compare your answer with the one on page 122.)

EXPERIMENT 5.7

Blood Evidence

Blood stains are often found at a crime scene, but how can an investigator be certain the stain is blood?

To test for blood an investigator might mix particles from the stain with phenolphthalein (an acid-base indicator) and hydrogen peroxide. Fizzing and a deep pink color indicates the presence of blood. Luminol can also be used. Luminol glows when in contact with dried blood and may reveal stains that were not noticed during a routine visual examination.

1. You can test for blood more easily. Prepare some sample stains for testing. Add a little water to separate medicine cups or vials that contain small amounts of red food coloring, ketchup, and tomato juice. In another cup or vial add a few drops of

animal blood that you can obtain from a butcher at a meat market or from raw beef purchased at such a market.

2. Add a few drops of each red solution to small pieces of cotton cloth. After the cloths dry, the stains should be evident.

3. To each stain add a drop of water. Wait a few seconds to allow some of the stain to dissolve. Then dip the reactive end of a Hemastix strip in the drop. What color do you observe on the strip when it touches blood?

If the stain is blood, further testing can determine whether it is human blood.

Human blood comes in different types. One type of designation is A, B, AB, or O. But typing information may or may not be useful. If the blood type matches that of the victim and that of the blood found on a knife in the possession of a suspect, then the knife *could have been* used in the crime. However, it is not positive proof. If the blood type on the knife does *not* match that of the victim, then we know the knife was *not* used on the victim. Or if it was, it was cleaned before being used on someone else.

Blood types are inherited. Since genes come in pairs (one on each pair of chromosomes), every person carries two genes for blood type. The genes that transmit blood type from one generation to the next can be represented by the letters *A*, *B*, and *o*. The lower case *o* is used to indicate that the gene is recessive. The capitalized *A* and *B* indicate codominant genes. Both *A* and *B* genes are dominant to *o* but not to each other. If a person has both the *A* and *B* genes, his or her blood type will be AB, the rarest type. Only 3 percent of the United States population are type AB (see Table 4). If someone has both recessive genes, *o* and *o*, his or her blood type will be type O, the most common blood type. A person who has type-A blood carries two genes for *A*, or one gene for type A plus the recessive gene *o*.

Blood types can be important in questions of paternity. Over half a century ago, an actress (Joan Barry) claimed that Charlie Chaplin, a well-known actor and comedian, was the father of her child.

The blood tests showed conclusively that Chaplin was not the child's father. Chaplin was type O. Barry was type A. The child was type B. Since neither Chaplin nor Barry carried the gene for type-B blood, Chaplin could not have been the father. Nonetheless, Chaplin was ordered to pay child support because in 1945 courts in California did not consider blood tests convincing evidence.

Blood Type	Percentage of the Population with that Blood Type
AB	3
B	9
A	42
O	46

TABLE 4: Percentage of the Population that Is of Each Blood Type

What blood types might be found in the children of two parents if both are type O?

What blood types might be found in the children of two parents if one parent is type A and the other is type B? (Compare your answers with the ones on page 123.)

Of course, blood types cannot prove paternity. For example, if the mother, baby, and the man accused of being the father are all type O, all that can be concluded is that the man *could* be the father of the child. Where blood tests are inconclusive, DNA testing, which is more expensive, can be used to determine paternity.

Spatter Science: Blood Drops and Splashes

A pattern of blood drops found at a crime scene may enable a forensic scientist to recreate the crime. By observing the dried drops, an expert can determine the angle and speed at which the drops struck a surface.

You can carry out experiments to see how the splash patterns of drops of "blood" are affected by height, horizontal speed, and angle.

YOU WILL NEED

- CUP
- WATER
- RED FOOD COLORING
- BASEMENT, GARAGE, OR OUTDOORS
- DROPPER
- WHITE PAPER
- RULER OR TAPE MEASURE
- TAPE
- CARDBOARD
- BLOCKS

1. Make a cup of water look like blood by adding some red food coloring to the water.

2. To avoid staining floors, take the "blood" to a basement, garage, or outdoor area on a day when there is no wind. Let drops from a dropper fall onto a sheet of white paper from different heights—2 cm (1 in), 15 cm (6 in), 30 cm (1 ft),

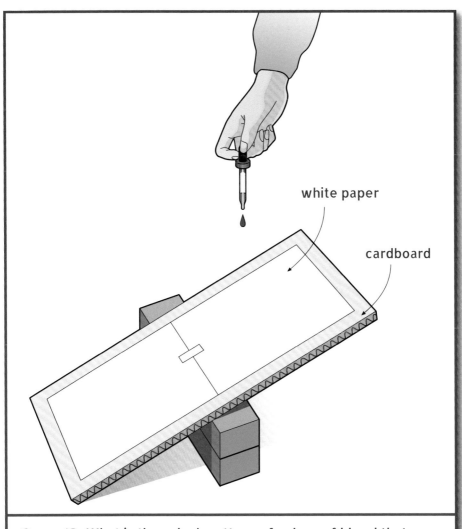

white paper

cardboard

FIGURE 12: What is the splash pattern of a drop of blood that strikes a surface at an angle?

100 cm (3.3 ft), and 150 cm (5 ft). How does the drop's splash pattern change with height?

3. Tape several sheets of paper together end to end. Let drops fall onto the paper as you move the dropper sideways above the paper. Do this from different heights. How does the drop's splash pattern change as the sideways speed of the dropper increases?

4. To see the effect of angle, tape several sheets of paper to a piece of cardboard. Raise one end of the cardboard by placing it on some blocks as shown in Figure 12. Let drops fall from different heights onto the incline. What do the splash patterns look like? What happens to the splash pattern of the drops if the incline is made steeper? Less steep?

Studying Hair Evidence

Hair has three layers (see Figure 13). The outer layer (cuticle) is a single layer of scalelike cells. The middle layer (cortex) is made up of long, narrow cells that usually contain pigment (color). The central layer (medulla) is a tube through the cortex. It contains many-sided cells arranged in rows.

YOU WILL NEED

- PEOPLE WHO WILL SUPPLY HAIR SAMPLES
- ENVELOPES
- PEN OR PENCIL
- DOG OR CAT
- TWEEZERS
- MAGNIFIER
- MICROSCOPE (IF AVAILABLE)
- PAPER
- A FRIEND

Looking through a microscope, you can see that human hair is clearly different from animal hair. The medulla of an animal's hair is continuous. In human hair, the medulla is often divided or unclear. The medulla index, the ratio of the diameter of the medulla to the diameter of the whole hair, can distinguish animal from human hair. The medulla, where it exists, is narrower in human hair—usually less than one-third the diameter of the hair. In animal

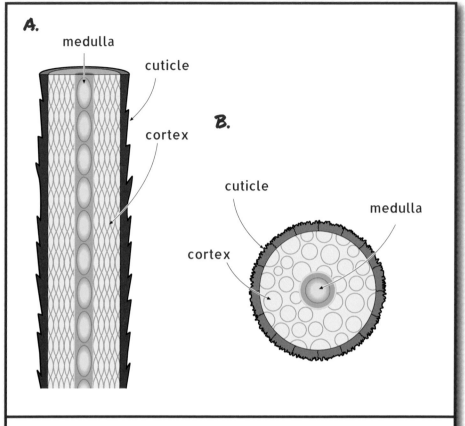

A.
medulla
cuticle
cortex

B.
cuticle
medulla
cortex

FIGURE 13: Magnified views of a hair: a) A longitudinal (side) view; b) A cross-sectional (end-on) view.

hair, the medulla is usually at least half the diameter of the hair.

1. Ask several people to give you samples of their hair. They can obtain hairs from their combs or hairbrushes, or they can pull one or more hairs from their scalps. If possible obtain hair samples from different racial groups—Caucasian, Asian,

African American. Place the samples in labeled envelopes so you know from whom each sample came. Also include samples from a dog or cat.

2. Remove a hair from an envelope using tweezers. Examine each sample using a microscope or a very powerful magnifier. Make a sketch of each kind of hair and any distinguishing features you observe. Do you see differences between human and animal hairs? If so, what are they? Are there observable differences in the hair samples from Caucasian, Asian, and African-American individuals? If so, what are they?

3. Without identifying the source, have a friend obtain another sample from one of the people who donated before. Examine and compare the unknown hair with the known samples. Can you identify from whom the hair came?

Studying Fiber Evidence

1. Collect samples of different types of cloth—cotton, wool, nylon, rayon, and others. Pull fibers from each of the cloths. Using tweezers, place the fibers in separate plastic containers. Label the containers according to the source of the fibers.

2. Examine each kind of fiber using a magnifier and then, if available, a microscope. In what ways do the fibers differ?

3. While you are not looking, have someone remove a few fibers from one of the cloths. Examine the unknown fibers with your magnifier or microscope. Can you tell from which cloth they came? If not, try examining them side by side with each known fiber. Can you identify the source of the unknown fibers?

Even the cleverest criminals often leave hair or fiber

YOU WILL NEED

- DIFFERENT TYPES OF CLOTH—COTTON, WOOL, NYLON, RAYON, AND OTHERS
- TWEEZERS
- SMALL PLASTIC CONTAINERS
- PEN OR PENCIL
- MAGNIFIER
- MICROSCOPE (IF AVAILABLE)

evidence behind. Forensic scientists compare fiber samples found at a crime scene with samples connected to a suspect by examining them under a comparison microscope. They compare color, diameter, and cross section. They also carry out chemical tests.

Fiber evidence was used by police in England to solve the 1968 murder of Claire Josephs. Mrs. Josephs was wearing a red woolen dress when she was killed. When they examined the suit of a suspect, they found a number of red wool fibers that matched those from Mrs. Josephs's dress. The carpet on the floor of the suspect's car contained fibers identical to those on Mrs. Josephs's carpet. This fiber evidence, along with blood stains taken from the suspect's car that matched the victim's blood type, led to a conviction.

CHAPTER 6

Crimes With Documents

How good are you at identifying handwriting? Were the words on a ransom note written by the suspected kidnapper? Was the signature on a check forged? Is a hundred-dollar bill counterfeit? These are the kinds of questions that forensic document examiners face as they study disputed documents.

Is It Real or Counterfeit?

How can you tell if the currency you receive is real or counterfeit? Since 1996, the United States Treasury has made copying currency and making counterfeit bills very difficult.

YOU WILL NEED

- AN ADULT
- $20 BILL
- STRONG MAGNIFYING LENS
- BLANK CHECK
- ERASER
- DROPPER
- BLEACH
- PHOTOCOPIER

1. Examine a twenty-dollar bill dated after 1996. Notice that the portrait of President Jackson on the front of the bill is detailed and off-center. A watermark (translucent image made by an impression when the bill was made) of Jackson's face is visible near the right side of the bill. The watermark can be seen from either side when the bill is held up to the light.

2. Within Jackson's portrait are a series of concentric lines that are very difficult to copy. The number indicating the value of the bill in the lower, right-hand corner appears green or gold when viewed head-on but darkens when viewed at an angle. Micro-printing of "USA 20," which is very difficult to duplicate, can be found within the number *20* in the lower, left-hand corner of the note. The print is so small that it cannot be read without being magnified. Similar microprinting of "United States of America" can be found to the right of the *20*. If you look carefully, you can see "TWENTY USA" written right side up and upside down and perpendicular to all the other printing near the left-hand edge of the bill. With a magnifier, you can find a few small blue and red fibers within the paper.

3. Ask your parent or guardian if you may borrow a blank personal check for an experiment. Examine the check to see how banks make forging checks difficult. Is the check colored? Examine the signature line with a strong magnifying lens. It probably has microprint so small that without magnification it looks like a line. What happens if you try to erase print on the check? **Ask an adult** to add a small drop of bleach to some print on the check. What happens?

4. Examine the security information on the back of the check. Photocopy both the front and back of the check. Does the security information appear when you photocopy the back of the check? What happens to the signature line when you photocopy the check?

Indented Writing Evidence

1. The next time your parent or guardian makes a shopping list, ask him or her to use a ballpoint pen on a pad of paper. After removing the top sheet that has the list, examine the sheet directly beneath. You can probably see the words in the shopping list as indented writing on the second sheet. You may see the writing more easily if you look at it from different angles. Another way to improve visibility is to slide the side of a pencil with soft lead gently back and forth across the indentations.

2. Once you have examined the indented writing carefully, recite the shopping list to the person who wrote it. How many items were you able to read?

Indented writing may provide valuable evidence if found as a page that was under a ransom note, instructions about a robbery, or a bookmaker's betting records.

Even faint indentations can be seen if an electrostatic

YOU WILL NEED

- PARENT OR GUARDIAN
- BALLPOINT PEN
- PAD OF PAPER
- PENCIL WITH SOFT LEAD

detection apparatus (ESDA) is used. Compressing paper changes its electrical properties. As a result, ESDA can detect indented writing. The document is placed on a metal plate and covered with a sheet of mylar. An electric field is applied to the apparatus. Then the mylar is sprayed with a mixture of toner and fine glass particles. The mixture sticks to the charged portions, making the indented words visible.

In 1988, the U.S. Secret Service used ESDA to investigate scientific fraud for a congressional committee. Their tests showed that laboratory data recorded in a notebook, supposedly in sequence, actually came from experiments conducted two years apart.

Handwriting Evidence

Handwriting, just like fingerprints, is unique, but much more difficult to identify. Even handwriting experts cannot be certain that a document was written by a suspect. To provide their

best opinion, they examine as many documents as possible, preferably lengthy ones in order to determine the suspect's natural style.

Documents that are crime related are often written crudely, in an unnatural style, or in a deliberately different style to avoid the subconscious movements that characterize a person's normal writing. Furthermore, everyone's handwriting changes with age and under the influence of alcohol or other drugs.

1. Write your name twice on a sheet of paper. Then write it again on a separate sheet and give it to a friend. Ask your friend to "forge" your signature by copying it on a separate sheet of paper.

2. Place a sheet of tracing paper over the two signatures that you kept. Do a top-of-letter analysis of both signatures. Make a dot on the tracing paper at the high point of each letter in your signature. Then connect the dots to form a pattern as shown in Figure 14a.

3. Use the tracing paper to do a bottom-of-letter analysis of both signatures. See Figure 14b.

4. Finally, use the tracing paper to do a slant analysis of your signatures as shown in Figure 14c. Are the patterns for your two signatures very similar?

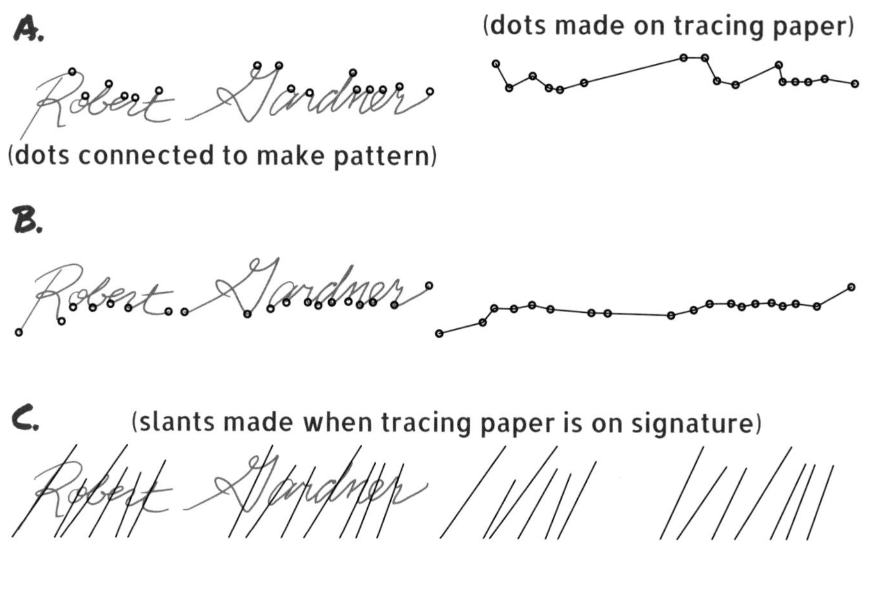

FIGURE 14: These techniques are used to analysze a signature.

5. Analyze the forged signature created by your friend in the same way. Could your analyses be used to convince a jury that the signature was forged? Why or why not?

Handwriting experts use the methods you have just used to analyze handwriting. They also look for the quality of the pen line. Is it smooth, tremulous, or jagged? Are there pauses, odd lifts of the pen, or flourishes (sweeping lines)? Are letters linked or do they have spaces between them? How are complex letters such as *b*s, *k*s, *g*s, and *q*s made? Are they looped or straight? Is there evidence of an unusual style?

6. Collect some signed writing samples from friends and members of your family. Then ask that they select someone from the group to write an unsigned note. See if you can determine who wrote the unsigned note.

Sometimes burning or spilled ink obscures the print on a document. In some cases, infrared light can make the print visible.

IDEA FOR YOUR SCIENCE FAIR

Collect handwriting samples from several people. Use the techniques you have learned to analyze the writing and to show how such analyses reveal differences in the way people write.

EVEN EXPERTS CAN BE FOOLED: THE HITLER DIARIES

In 1983, Gerd Heidemann, a German citizen, claimed he had access to Adolf Hitler's diaries. A company agreed to pay $6 million for the documents if they were real. Several handwriting experts compared the documents with known samples of Hitler's writing. They all agreed that Hitler wrote the diaries.

Later, forensic scientists discovered that the paper in the diaries had not been produced until after World War II. Furthermore, the inks in the documents and the threads in the binder were not sold until after the war in 1945.

It turned out that Konrad Kujau, a known forger of art and Nazi memorabilia, had written the diaries in 1980. Both Heidemann and Kujau were sent to prison.

Ink Evidence

1. You can use a technique known as chromatography to separate the colored chemicals used in inks. To see how this is done, collect a number of different colored marking pens as well as blue and black ink pens. Then cut some strips about 2 cm x 15 cm (1 in x 6 in) from white coffee filters, filter paper, or white blotter paper.

2. About 2 cm (1 in) from one end of a paper strip, make a stripe using one of the pens you collected. Label the other end of the paper strip so you can identify the pen used to make the stripe. Do the

YOU WILL NEED

- AN ADULT
- SEVERAL DIFFERENT COLORED MARKING PENS
- BLUE AND BLACK INK PENS
- SCISSORS
- WHITE COFFEE FILTERS, FILTER PAPER, OR BLOTTER PAPER
- PENCIL
- FOOD COLORINGS (OPTIONAL)
- TOOTHPICKS
- KITCHEN CUPBOARD OR RULER
- BOOKS OR BRICKS
- WATER
- WIDE CONTAINER
- LARGE, TALL, CLEAR JAR OR CYLINDER
- ALUMINUM FOIL
- RUBBING ALCOHOL
- SOMEONE TO WRITE A MESSAGE USING ONE OF THE PENS YOU COLLECTED
- SHARP KNIFE

same for each pen. You might also use food colorings. Use a toothpick to paint the food coloring stripes.

3. When the strips are dry, hang the paper strips from a kitchen cupboard or from a ruler supported by books or bricks as shown in Figure 15a. The bottom ends of the strips should just touch the water in a wide container. Capillarity (the rise of water in the narrow spaces between the paper fibers) will cause the water to slowly "climb" up the paper, carrying the colored chemicals with it. Do any of the inks become separated into different colored pigments? Which inks can you identify from the chromatograms you have made?

4. If the air is very dry, the water may evaporate from the paper strips before separation of the colored chemicals is complete. If that is the case, repeat the experiment in a large, tall, clear jar or cylinder such as the one shown in Figure 15b. Cover the top of the jar with aluminum foil.

5. Some of the inks may not move with the water. These inks are insoluble in water, but they may be soluble in alcohol. For those inks, repeat the experiment using rubbing alcohol. Because alcohol evaporates rapidly, this part of the experiment should be done in a closed container such as the one shown in Figure 15b.

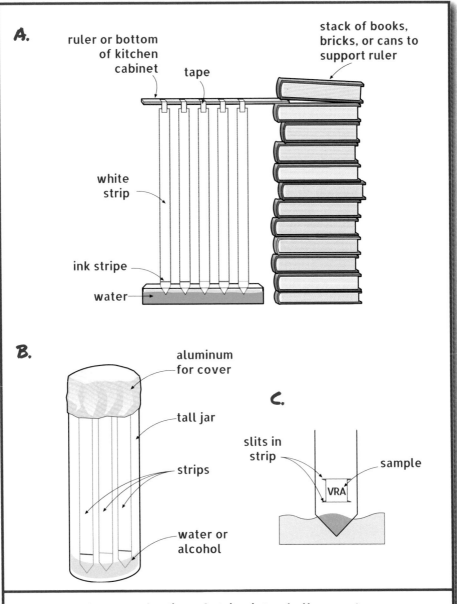

A.

ruler or bottom of kitchen cabinet

tape

stack of books, bricks, or cans to support ruler

white strip

ink stripe

water

B.

aluminum for cover

tall jar

strips

water or alcohol

C.

slits in strip

sample

VRA

FIGURE 15: a) Lower the tips of strips into shallow water.
b) Cover a jar or cylinder for use in dry air. c) Cut slits in a strip to hold a writing sample from an unknown pen.

6. Have someone, in your absence, write a message using one of the pens you collected. Cut a sample from the writing. **Ask an adult** to use a sharp knife to cut two slits in a paper strip. Insert the sample between the slits as shown in Figure 15c.

7. Using the chromatographic technique, try to separate the ink into its colored components using water or alcohol. Can you identify the pen that was used to write the note?

Crime laboratories often use chromatography to compare inks found at a crime scene with inks found in the pen of a suspect. An International Ink Library, under the control of the U.S. Secret Service, has information about the chemicals in thousands of inks. The Bureau of Alcohol, Tobacco, Firearms, and Explosives can provide chromatography information about several thousand inks. These chromatographs can be compared with chromatographs made from inks used as evidence. Such comparisons have proved that dated documents actually used ink made long after the time they were supposedly written.

Piecing It Back Together

Sometimes criminals leave torn papers that can be used as evidence.

YOU WILL NEED

- PARENT OR GUARDIAN
- WASTEBASKET
- TORN DOCUMENTS

1. Ask a parent or guardian for permission to examine the contents of a wastebasket. Search for documents that have been torn. If there are none, tear some discarded papers into several pieces.

2. Try to reassemble the torn documents. You might begin by separating glossy paper from the rest. Then select large pieces of paper followed by smaller pieces. Finally, try to piece the documents back together so their contents can be read. What types of crime might be solved using this method?

Using Invisible Inks

For more than a thousand years criminals and others have used invisible inks to avoid detection of messages. During the American Revolution, George Washington used invisible ink to send messages that might have been intercepted by British troops.

YOU WILL NEED

- AN ADULT
- TOOTHPICKS
- LEMON JUICE
- WHITE PAPER
- STOVE
- TINCTURE OF IODINE
- DROPPER
- MEASURING CUP
- SAUCER
- NEWSPAPER
- WATER

There are two kinds of invisible ink, organic and sympathetic. Organic inks are natural substances such as lemon juice, vinegar, milk, even saliva. These inks become visible when heated. Sympathetic inks turn colorless as they dry. They are made visible by applying a chemical. For example, a message written with a weak acid can be made visible by applying an acid-base indicator such as diluted grape juice.

1. Print an invisible message of your own. Use a tooth-pick as a pen and lemon juice as ink to write a message on a sheet of white paper.

2. After the lemon juice has dried, **ask an adult** to carefully move the paper back and forth over a hot stove burner. The heat will decompose the organic chemicals in the dry lemon juice forming a visible "ink" that will allow you to read the message.

3. You can also use lemon juice as a sympathetic invisible ink. Write another message on a small piece of white paper. While the message is drying, place two drops of tincture of iodine in a saucer. Put the saucer on a newspaper. Then add 30 mL ($^1/_8$ cup) of water to the saucer.

4. When the message has dried, dip the paper into the iodine solution in the saucer. The paper will turn blue because it contains starch. The citric acid that was in the lemon juice reacts with iodine to form a clear substance. Thus, your message will appear as clear letters on a dark background, at least for a short time.

Can You Break the Codes?

Criminals, terrorists, and spies sometimes communicate by using codes. Examples of simple codes are shown in Table 5.

Devise one or more codes of your own. Have small groups of friends or classmates write messages in a code that they devise. Then have the groups "intercept" one another's messages. Can the intercepting group decode the messages they intercept?

Example 1: Each letter is assigned a number.

a is 1, b is 2, c is 3, . . . x is 24, y is 25, z is 26.

Example 2: Each letter is assigned a number, but in reverse order of example 1.

a is 26, b is 25, c is 24 . . . x is 3, y is 2, z is 1.

Example 3: Each letter is assigned two numbers as shown below, first by column and then by row. a is 11, b is 21, c is 31 . . . x is 35, y is 45, z is 55. Notice that u and v are both 15.

	1	2	3	4	5
1	a	b	c	d	e
2	f	g	h	i	j
3	k	l	m	n	o
4	p	q	r	s	t
5	uv	w	x	y	z

Example 4: A message could be written in an up-down sequence. "Read this message" would be written as:

ratimsae   or as   ra ti msae

edhsesg   ed hs esg

Example 5: A simple code would be to write words backwards and in reverse order. "Read this message" would be written as: egassem siht daer.

Example 6: Messages could be written using mirror writing; that is, the writing could be read by holding it in front of a mirror. Leonardo da Vinci's notebooks were written entirely in this code.

TABLE 5: Examples of Some Codes

Answers to Some Questions in this Book

List of observed errors in Figure 1: The **pitcher** has his hat on backwards, he has no glove on his hand, he is holding a football not a baseball, and he has no socks or shoes on his feet.

The **batter** is wearing a cap indicating a New York team, but his shirt suggests he is a Boston Red Sox player, except that the words are reversed. His socks do not match, nor do his shoes, and, being a right-handed batter, his batting hands should have the right hand above the left, not the reverse as shown.

The **catcher**, who is not wearing a mask, is sitting on a stool. He has a glove on his right hand, indicating that he throws with his left hand (no professional catchers throw left-handed), and he is not trying to hide his signals to the pitcher. Normally, catchers give hand signals to the pitcher with their hand between their thighs, so the opposing team cannot see the signs. Finally, home plate is turned the wrong way. The wide part should be away from the catcher.

In Figure 11, suspect AME must have been at the crime scene. That suspect's DNA matches that found at the crime scene.

Blood types: If both parents have type-O blood, both have two recessive genes (*o* and *o*); therefore, all their children will have type-O blood.

If one parent is type A and the other type B, the genes the type-A parent carries might be *A* and *A,* or *A* and *o*. The genes the type-B parent carries might be *B* and *B,* or *B* and *o*. Consequently, their children could be any of the four blood types—A, B, AB, or O.

Appendix:
Science Supply Companies

Arbor Scientific
P.O. Box 2750
Ann Arbor, MI 48106-2750
(800) 367-6695
arborsci.com

Carolina Biological Supply Co.
P.O. Box 6010
Burlington, NC 27216-6010
(800) 334-5551
carolina.com

Connecticut Valley Biological Supply Co., Inc.
82 Valley Road, Box 326
Southampton, MA 01073
(800) 628-7748
ctvalleybio.com

Delta Education
P.O. Box 3000
80 Northwest Blvd.
Nashua, NH 03061-3000
(800) 258-1302
delta-education.com

Edmund Scientifics
532 Main Street
Tonawanda, NY 14150-6711
(800) 818-4955
scientificsonline.com

Educational Innovations, Inc.
5 Francis J. Clarke Circle
Bethel, CT 06801
(203) 748-3224
teachersource.com

Fisher Science
300 Industry Drive
Pittsburgh, PA 15275
(800) 766-7000
new.fishersci.com

Nasco
P.O. Box 901
901 Janesville Avenue
Fort Atkinson, WI 53538-0901
(800) 558-9595
enasco.com

Sargent-Welch/VWR Scientific
P.O. Box 92912
Rochester, NY 14692-9012
(800) 727-4368
SargentWelch.com

Ward's Science
P.O. Box 92912
5100 West Henrietta Road
Rochester, NY 14692-9012
(800) 962-2660
wardsci.com

Further Reading

BOOKS

Churchill, E. Richard, Louis V. Loeschnig, and Muriel Mandell. *365 Simple Science Experiments With Everyday Materials.* New York: Black Dog & Leventhal Publishers, 2013.

Dutton, Judy. *Science Fair Season: Twelve Kids, a Robot Named Scorch, and What It Takes to Win.* New York: Hyperion Books, 2011.

Editors of TIME for Kids Magazine. *TIME For Kids Big Book of Science Experiments: A Step-by-Step Guide.* New York: TIME for Kids, 2011.

Henneberg, Susan. *Creating Science Fair Projects With Cool New Digital Tools.* New York: Rosen Publishing, 2014.

Margles, Samantha. *Mythbusters Science Fair Book.* New York: Scholastic, 2011.

Woog, Adam. *Careers in Forensic Science.* New York: Cavendish Square Publishing, 2014.

WEB SITES

all-about-forensic-science.com
Scientist interviews, facts, and links about many forensic science topics, including fingerpinting, DNA, and ballistics.

fbi.gov/fun-games/kids/kids
Visit the Kids Page at the Federal Bureau of Investigation.

ipl.org/div/projectguide
The IPL's Science Fair Project Resource Guide will help guide you through your science fair project.

Index

A

American Revolution, 118
arches, 27, 28
arsenic, 45–46
automated fingerprints
  identification system (AFIS),
  29

B

Barry, Joan, 94
BATF, 116
blood evidence
  blood types, 67, 93–95
  splash patterns, 96–98
  testing for, 92–93
Bonaparte, Napoleon, 46
bones, 68–71
branching grooves, 39

C

capillarity, 114
cause of death determination,
  73–75
Chaplin, Charlie, 94
chemistry lab station, 16
chromatography, 113–116
chromosomes, 83
combination patterns, 27, 28
crime lab, building principles,
  11–12
currency, counterfeit, 105–106
cyanoacrylate (Super Glue), 33,
  35–36

D

decomposition, 76–79
diamond grooves, 39
diatoms, 74–75
diazafluoren (DFO), 33
DNA evidence
  forensic typing, 83–88
  human remains
    identification, 71–72
  PCR, 84–88
  profiling, 89–91
  short tandem repeats, 86–87
document analysis
  check forging, 106
  codes, 120–121
  currency, counterfeit, 105–106
  ink, 113–116
  ink, invisible, 118–119
  lab station, 15
  torn paper, 117
  writing, indented, 107–108
drowning, 73–75

E

ear witnesses, 23
electrophoresis, 89–91
electrostatic detection apparatus
  (ESDA), 108
eyewitnesses, 21–22

F

Federal Bureau of Investigation
  (FBI), 29, 61, 88
fiber evidence, 102–103

fingerprints
    classifying, 27–29
    dusting, 32
    identifying, 30
    lab station, 13
    latent, lifting, 31–33
    latent, viewing, 35–37
    points of similarity, 29
    recording, 25–26
    stability of, 25
footprints, 40–42
forensic science, 5
forgery, 106, 109–112

G

gender determination, 68–69
genes, 93–94
glass analysis
    density, 54–57, 63
    lab station, 14
    pieces, matching, 53–54
    refractivity, 59–64

H

hair evidence, 99–101
handwriting analysis, 109–112
Hayashi, Masumi/Kenji, 46
Heidemann, Gerd, 112
height estimation, 69–71
Hitler, Adolf, 112
Hitler's diaries, 112
human remains
    drowning, 73–75
    identification, 71–72
    temperature, 80–83
hydrogen peroxide, 92

I

immersion testing, 52–64
ink analysis, 113–116
insulation, 82–83
International Ink Library, 116
iodine, 33, 49, 119

J

Josephs, Claire, 103

K

Kujau, Konrad, 112

L

Lafarge, Marie, 45–46
lip prints, 38–39
Locard, Edmond, 5
loops, 27, 28
luminol, 92

M

Marsh, James, 45
Marsh test, 45–46
Mengele, Josef, 71–72
micro-printing, 105–106
moisture, 78
mold, 78–79

N

ninhydrin, 33

O

observational skills
    ear witnesses, 23
    eyewitnesses, 21–22
    overview, 17

sight, 18
smell, touch, taste, hearing, 19–20
Orfila, Mathieu J. B., 46
organic inks, 118

P

paternity, 94–95
PCR, 84–88
pencil lasers, 43–44
phenolphthalein, 92
photography, 32, 40
place of death determination, 73–75
plaster of Paris, 40–42

R

rectangular grooves, 39
refractivity
    glass analysis, 59–64
    immersion testing, 52–64
    principles, 59–61

S

safety, 9–10, 33, 43, 49, 78–79
scars in fingerprints, 27, 28
science fairs, 6–8
scientific fraud, 108
scientific method, 8–9
short tandem repeats (STRs), 86–87
signatures analysis, 109–112
silicone oil, 62–64
silver nitrate, 33
substance analysis
    appearance, feel, 48

conductivity, 50–52
heat testing, 49–50
iodine testing, 49
sample preparation, 47
solubility, 48–49
test results record, 48
vinegar testing, 50
sympathetic inks, 118

T

teeth impressions, 66–67
time of death determination, 76–83
tire prints, 40–42
transference principle, 5, 53

U

U.S. Secret Service, 108

V

vertical grooves, 39
voice prints, 43–44

W

Washington, George, 118
watermarks, 105
whorls, 27, 28
writing, indented, 107–108